The Thousand Names of
Vishnu

VIJAYA KUMAR

A Sterling Paperbacks

STERLING PAPERBACKS
An imprint of
Sterling Publishers (P) Ltd.
A-59 Okhla Industrial Area, Phase-II,
New Delhi-110020.
Tel: 26387070, 26386209; Fax: 91-11-26383788
E-mail: ghai@nde.vsnl.net.in
www.sterlingpublishers.com

The Thousand Names of Vishnu
Copyright © 2006 by Sterling Publishers Pvt. Ltd.
ISBN 978 81 207 3009 0
Reprint 2008

Published by Sterling Publishers Pvt. Ltd., New Delhi-110 020.
Printed at Sterling Publishers Pvt. Ltd., New Delhi-110020.

Preface

Sahasranama or the thousand names of a deity is perhaps the most extensive elaboration of the Divine Name. It is the most popular and the holiest form of the Divine Being.

Every name or *stotra* of the Divine Being is an invocation of a particular cult deity, like Vishnu, Shiva, Ganesha, and so on. These names, strung together into verses, indicate the inexhaustibility of the attributes and glories of that deity. The glories of God manifest themselves in many ways through the sentient and the insentient, and by chanting these names, the devotees show their adoration for the Lord. These names create the holy link with their Maker.

The thousand names of Shiva were first chanted by Krishna for the benefit of Yudhishthira in the presence of Bhishma. Then came the thousand names of Vishnu by Bhishma to Yudhishthira in Krishna's presence on the same occasion. Since Ganesha is the Lord of all obstacles, and is the one whose worship is foremost, his thousand names came into being.

Each of these books need not necessarily contain exactly thousand names. The numbers may be increased or decreased according to the devotee's choice. What matters ultimately is that these names are the shortest expressions of the profoundest meanings.

1. Vishwam: *The All*

ॐ विश्वस्मै नमः

Lord Vishnu is the Universe, the supreme Brahman.

2. Vishnu: *The All-pervading*

ॐ विष्णवे नमः

Lord Vishnu pervades the whole universe, externally and internally.

3. Vashatakara: *The Holy Expression —Vashat*

ॐ वषटकाराय नमः

Sacrifice, indeed, is Vishnu, and on His account, *Vashatakara* (oblations) are offered.

4. Bhutabhavya Bhavatprabhu: *The Lord Of The Past, Present And Future*

ॐ भूतभव्यभवत्प्रभवे नमः

He is beyond time, is eternal and undecayed.

5. Bhutakrut: *The Creator Of All Beings*

ॐ भूतकृते नमः

He creates and destroys all existences in the universe.

6. Bhutabhrut: *The Supporter Of Beings*

ॐ भूतभृते नमः

He sustains and governs the universe.

7. Bhava: *Pure Existence*

ॐ भावाय नमः

He manifests Himself as the universe, or remains as pure Existence.

8. Bhutatma: *The Self Of Beings*

ॐ भूतात्मने नमः

He is the indweller residing in all beings.

9. Bhutabhavana: *The Generator Of Beings*

ॐ भूतभावनाय नमः

He generates and develops beings.

10. Putatma: *Pure Self*

ॐ पूतात्मने नमः

He is the Purity and Essence of all things.

11. Paramatma: *The Supreme Self*

ॐ परमात्मने नमः

He is pure and free Consciousness, and beyond cause and effect.

12. Muktanam Paramagati: *The Supreme Goal Of The Liberated*

ॐ मुक्तानां परमायै गतये नमः

One who attains to Him, is never reborn, for there is nothing higher than Him.

13. Avyaya: *The Undecaying*

ॐ अव्ययाय नमः

He is unaging, undecaying, undying, immortal and indestructible.

14. Purusha: *The Spirit*

ॐ पुरूषाय नमः

He is the supreme Spirit residing in and pervading everything.

15. Sakshi: *The Witness*

ॐ साक्षिणे नमः

He witnesses everything by His own awareness and inherent nature.

16. Kshetrajna: *The Knower Of The Field*

ॐ क्षेत्रज्ञाय नमः

He knows the fields or bodies by His yogic powers.

17. Akshara: *Without Destruction*

ॐ अक्षराय नमः

As the supreme Spirit, He is the undecaying Self who cannot be destroyed.

18. Yoga: *One Attainable Through Yoga*

ॐ योगाय नमः

He is Yoga as He is to be reached by means of it.

19. Yogavidam Neta: *The Master Of Those Who Know Yoga*

ॐ योगविदां नेत्रे नमः

He is the Master of those who are established in Yoga.

20. Pradhana Purusheshvara: *The Lord Of Pradhana And Purusha*

ॐ प्रधानपुरुषेश्वराय नमः

He is the Lord of *Pradhana* (Primordial Nature) or *Maya* and *Purusha* (individual self or *jiva*).

21. Narasimhavapu: *The One With The Man-lion Form*

ॐ नारसिंहवपुषे नमः

In Him (as the Incarnation of Narasimha), the bodies of a man and a lion are combined.

22. Shriman: *On Whose Chest Resides Shri*

ॐ श्रीमते नमः

On His chest, the goddess Shri or Lakshmi eternally dwells.

23. Keshava: *Whose Hair Is Beautiful*

ॐ केशवाय नमः

His locks of hair are beautiful. Keshava also suggests He is the Trinity; or He, who destroyed the demon Keshi in the Krishna incarnation.

24. Purushottama: *The Highest Spirit*

ॐ पुरुषोत्तमाय नमः

He is the greatest among all spirits, as He is indestructible.

25. Sarva: *The All*

ॐ सर्वस्मै नमः

He is the omniscient source of all existence.

26. Sharva: *The Withdrawer*

ॐ शर्वाय नमः

He withdraws all beings during cosmic Dissolution, or causes to be withdrawn unto Himself.

27. Shiva: *The Pure*

ॐ शिवाय नमः

He is free from the three qualities of nature—*Sattva*, *Rajas* and *Tamas*—and hence pure. There is no difference between Vishnu and Shiva as He is One.

28. Sthanu: *The Immovable*

ॐ स्थाणवे नमः

He is immovable, steady and changeless.

29. Bhutadi: *The Source Of Beings*

ॐ भूतादये नमः

He is the first cause of beings, elements or existence.

30. Nidhi: *The Resting Place*

ॐ निधये नमः

He is the unchangeable resting place and indestructible Being remaining in seminal condition at the time of cosmic Dissolution.

31. Avyaya: *The Changeless*

ॐ अव्ययाय नमः

He remains unchangeable, even during Dissolution.

32. Sambhava: *The Source Of Birth*

ॐ संभवाय नमः

He is born out of His own will as incarnation.

33. Bhavana: *The Effecter*

ॐ भावनाय नमः

He generates the fruits of action among all *jivas*.

34. Bharta: *The Sustainer*

ॐ भर्त्रे नमः

He supports the universe as its substratum.

35. Prabhava: *The Birthplace*

ॐ प्रभवाय नमः

He is the source from whom all elements are born.

8

36. Prabhu: *The Most Powerful*

ॐ प्रभवे नमः

He is adept in all rites, showing it forth in all His actions.

37. Ishwara: *The Mighty*

ॐ ईश्वराय नमः

He has unlimited power over all things.

38. Swayambhu: *The Self-born*

ॐ स्वयंभुवे नमः

He is omnipresent and self-existent.

39. Shambhu: *The Bestower Of Happiness*

ॐ शंभवे नमः

He bestows happiness on his devotees.

40. Aditya: *The Sun*

ॐ आदित्याय नमः

He is the golden-hued Being in the sun's orb.

41. Pushkaraksha: *The Lotus-eyed*

ॐ पुष्कराक्षाय नमः

He has eyes resembling the petals of a lotus.

42. Mahasvana: *Of Mighty Sound*

ॐ महास्वनाय नमः

He is the holy sound, the eternal word from whom comes the great sound — the – Veda.

43. Anadinidhana: *Without Beginning And End*

ॐ अनादिनिधनाय नमः

He is Existence that has neither birth nor death.

44. Dhata: *The Supporter*

ॐ धात्रे नमः

He is the support of the universe.

45. Vidhata: *The Dispenser*

ॐ विधात्रे नमः

He generates or dispenses the fruit of action and induces action.

46. Dhaturuttama: *The Best Of All Constituents*

ॐ धातवे उत्तमाय नमः

As the ultimate support of everything, He is pure Consciousness.

47. Aprameya: *The Immeasurable*

ॐ अप्रमेयाय नमः

He is not measurable and is beyond the senses.

48. Hrishikesha: *The Lord Of The Senses*

ॐ हृषीकेशाय नमः

He controls the senses. Or, the word also means He has hair consisting of the rays of the sun and the moon, giving joy to the world.

49. Padmanabha: *Lotus-navelled*

ॐ पद्मनाभाय नमः

In His navel, He bears the lotus which symbolises the source of the universe.

50. Amaraprabhu: *The Lord Of The Immortals*

ॐ अमरप्रभवे नमः

He is the Lord of the devas who are immortal.

51. Vishvakarma: *The Creator Of The Universe*

ॐ विश्वकर्मणे नमः

His power of creation is unique.

52. Manu: *The Thinker*

ॐ मनवे नमः

There is no thinker except Him.

53. Tvashta: *The Reducer*

ॐ त्वष्ट्रे नमः

He reduces all beings during the withdrawal of the universe.

54. Sthavishta: *The Biggest*

ॐ स्थविष्ठाय नमः

He excels in everything in bulk or substantiality.

55. Sthavira Dhruva: *The Ancient And Firm*

ॐ स्थविराय ध्रुवाय नमः

He is the eternal One, being the most ancient and stable.

56. Agrahya: *He Who Cannot Be Grasped*

ॐ अग्राह्याय नमः

He is beyond the grasp of knowledge, from whom all speech, with mind, turns away, and is unable to reach it.

57. Shashvata: *Ever-existing*

ॐ शाश्वताय नमः

He is eternal, undecaying and auspicious.

58. Krishna: *The Existence-knowledge-bliss*

ॐ कृष्णाय नमः

Krish means existence and *na* means bliss. Lord Vishnu is the union of these two. He is also dark-complexioned.

59. Lohitaksha: *Red-eyed*

ॐ लोहिताक्षाय नमः

His eyes are tinged red.

60. Pratardana: *The Diminisher*

ॐ प्रतर्दनाय नमः

He diminishes all beings during the Dissolution of the world.

61. Prabhuta: *Well-endowed*

ॐ प्रभूताय नमः

He is well-endowed with omnipotence, omniscience, wisdom, greatness, etc.

62. Trikakubdhama: *The Support Of The Three Regions*

ॐ त्रिककुब्धाम्ने नमः

He supports the three regions, above, below and in the middle.

63. Pavitram: *The Holy*

ॐ पवित्राय नमः

He is the means of purification, for He purifies everything.

11

64. Mangalam Param: *The Supremely Auspicious*

ॐ मङ्गलाय परस्मै नमः

His very remembrance bestows the auspicious in abundance.

65. Ishana: *The Ruler*

ॐ ईशानाय नमः

He is the Ruler who controls and regulates everything.

66. Pranada: *The Bestower Of Vital Energy*

ॐ प्राणदाय नमः

He is the One who gives the Prana (the life), and destroys it.

67. Prana: *The Supreme Self*

ॐ प्राणाय नमः

He is the life-force behind the living soul of the individual.

68. Jyeshta Shreshta: *The Eldest And The Best*

ॐ ज्येष्ठ श्रेष्ठाय नमः

He is the eldest of all, there being none prior to Him.

69. Prajapati: *The Lord Of All Beings*

ॐ प्रजापतये नमः

He is the Master of all existence.

70. Hiranyagarbha: *The Self Of Even Brahma*

ॐ हिरण्यगर्भाय नमः

He is the Self of Brahma who is known as Hiranyagarbha that contains the whole universe in the seminal form.

71. Bhugarbha: *Having The Universe In Himself*

ॐ भूगर्भाय नमः

He is the large womb, holding the universe in Himself.

72. Madhava: *The Consort Of Lakshmi*

ॐ माधवाय नमः

As the consort of Lakshmi, He is recognised through silence, meditation and yoga (*Manu-vidya*).

73. Madhusudana: *The Slayer Of Madhu*

ॐ मधुसूदनाय नमः

He slew the dreaded demon, Madhu, at the request of Brahma.

74. Ishvara: *The Omnipotent*

ॐ ईश्वराय नमः

He is the Omnipotent, possessing the eight siddhis, and capable of becoming smaller than an atom.

75. Vikrami: *The Valiant*

ॐ विक्रमिणे नमः

He is the courageous One.

76. Dhanvi: *The Archer*

ॐ धन्विने नमः

He is the One (as Rama) armed with the bow.

77. Medhavi: *Of Great Intelligence*

ॐ मेधाविने नमः

He is capable of grasping all texts at any time.

78. Vikrama: *Of Great Strides*

ॐ विक्रमाय नमः

He, having great strides, traversed the universe; or He has the bird Garuda as His mount.

79. Krama: *The Walker*

ॐ क्रमाय नमः

He is the cause of movement.

80. Anuttama: *The Greatest*

ॐ अनुत्तमाय नमः

There is nothing above, below or equal to Him.

81. Duradharsha: *The Unassailable*

ॐ दुराधर्षाय नमः

He is One whom none can overcome.

13

82. Kritajna: *The Knower Of Actions Done*

ॐ कृतज्ञाय नमः

He knows everything about what has been done, whether good or bad.

83. Kriti: *The Effort*

ॐ कृतये नमः

As the universal Self, He is considered as the very basis of every act and effort.

84. Atmavan: *Centred In His Own Glory*

ॐ आत्मवते नमः

He is established in His own greatness.

85. Suresha: *The Lord Of Gods*

ॐ सुरेशाय नमः

He is the Lord of those who bestow good.

86. Sharanam: *The Refuge*

ॐ शरणाय नमः

He, as the Refuge, destroys the sorrow of the distressed.

87. Sharma: *Bliss*

ॐ शर्मणे नमः

He is supreme Bliss.

88. Vishvareta: *The Universal Cause*

ॐ विश्वरेतसे नमः

He is the seed of the universe, and hence the cause of all.

89. Prajabhava: *The Source Of All Beings*

ॐ प्रजाभवाय नमः

He is the source from whom all beings have originated.

90. Aha: *The Day*

ॐ अहे नमः

He is the Light, or the Day, for He is luminous.

91. Samvatsara: *The Year*

ॐ संवत्सराय नमः

In His aspect as Time, he is the year.

92. Vyala: *The Elusive*

ॐ व्यालाय नमः

He is like the Elephant or the Serpent, being ungraspable.

93. Pratyaya: *Consciousness*

ॐ प्रत्ययाय नमः

He is pure Consciousness.

94. Sarvadarshana: *The All-seeing*

ॐ सर्वदर्शनाय नमः

He has eyes everywhere as He is omnipresent.

95. Aja: *The Unborn*

ॐ अजाय नमः

He has no birth and would never be born.

96. Sarveshvara: *The Lord Of All Lords*

ॐ सर्वेश्वराय नमः

He is the Lord of all.

97. Siddha: *The Perfect*

ॐ सिद्धाय नमः

Being ever established in His own nature, He is eternally perfect.

98. Siddhi: *The Consciousness In All Things*

ॐ सिद्धये नमः

As He is imperishable, He is the consciousness in all things, and has a form that excels all.

99. Sarvadi: *The Beginning Of All*

ॐ सर्वादये नमः

He is the origin or first cause of all beings or elements.

100. Achyuta: *The Unlapsing*

ॐ अच्युताय नमः

He is ceaseless, for He has not lapsed, is not lapsing, and will not lapse.

101. Vrishakapi: *Dharma And The Boar*

ॐ वृषाकपये नमः

He, as Dharma, showers all objects of desire, and as the Boar (or Varaha incarnation) He saved the earth from the deluge.

102. Ameyatma: *Of Undefinable Nature*

ॐ अमेयात्मने नमः

His form or nature cannot be measured and determined.

103. Sarvayogavinihsrita: *Devoid Of All Bondages*

ॐ सर्वयोगविनिःसृताय नमः

He is without any attachment. It also can mean One who is known all the Yogas.

104. Vasu: *The Dweller*

ॐ वसवे नमः

He is the One in whom all beings dwell and who dwells in all.

105. Vasumana: *Of Great Mind*

ॐ वसुमनसे नमः

He is One possessed of a great mind, free from attachments and pollution.

106. Satya: *The Truth*

ॐ सत्याय नमः

He is Truth, Knowledge and the Infinite.

107. Samatma: *The Same Self*

ॐ समात्मने नमः

He is present alike in all beings.

108. Asammita: *Unlimited*

ॐ असंमिताय नमः

He is unlimited by any entity.

109. Sama: *The Same At All Times*

ॐ समाय नमः

He is imperturbed at all times, and is the same in all beings.

110. Amogha: *Of Fruitful Worship*

ॐ अमोघाय नमः

He is One whose worship will never go in vain.

111. Pundarikaksha: *Pervading The Lotus Of The Heart*

ॐ पुण्डरीकाक्षाय नमः

Having lotus-like eyes, He is the lotus in the centre of the body.

112. Vrushakarma: *Of Righteous Action*

ॐ वृषकर्मणे नमः

His actions are according to Dharma.

113. Vrishakriti: *Incarnated For Establishing Dharma*

ॐ वृषाकृतये नमः

For the sake of establishing righteousness, He incarnates in every age.

114. Rudra: *The Destroyer Of Misery*

ॐ रुद्राय नमः

He removes all sorrows, confers goodness, and causes all beings to cry during cosmic Dissolution.

115. Bahushira: *Myriad-headed*

ॐ बहुशिरसे नमः

He has innumerable heads.

116. Babhru: *The Supporter Of The World*

ॐ बभ्रवे नमः

He governs and supports the world.

117. Vishvayoni: *The Universal Cause*

ॐ विश्वयोनये नमः

He is the cause of the world.

17

118. Shuchishrava: *Of Holy Names*

ॐ शुचिश्रवसे नमः

His names are holy and worthy of being heard.

119. Amruta: *The Immortal*

ॐ अमृताय नमः

He has no death or decay, and is ageless.

120. Shashvatasthanu: *Eternally Firm*

ॐ शाश्वतस्थाणवे नमः

He is unchanging, firmly established and eternal.

121. Vararoha: *Of Excellent Ascent*

ॐ वरारोहाय नमः

He is the supreme Goal whom aspirants try to reach and ascend, never to return for rebirth.

122. Mahatapa: *Of Sublime Austerity*

ॐ महातपसे नमः

His *tapas* (austerity) is of the nature of knowledge, and his glory and greatness are supreme.

123. Sarvaga: *The All-pervading*

ॐ सर्वगाय नमः

He pervades everything as the universal cause.

124. Sarvavidbhanu: *The Omniscient Sun*

ॐ सर्वविद्भानवे नमः

He is omniscient, illumining everything with effulgence.

125. Vishwaksena: *Before Whom Armies Flee*

ॐ विष्वक्सेनाय नमः

By merely preparing for the fight, He routs the armies, and protects His devotees.

126. Janardana: *The Chastiser Of The Wicked*

ॐ जनार्दनाय नमः

He inflicts suffering on the wicked, and devotees pray to Him for worldly success and liberation.

127. Veda: *The Embodiment Of Scriptures*

ॐ वेदाय नमः

He destroys the darkness, born of ignorance by bestowing knowledge.

128. Vedavit: *The Knower Of The Vedas*

ॐ वेदविदे नमः

He is the author of the *Vedanta* and the knower of the Vedas.

129. Avyanga: *The Perfect*

ॐ अव्यङ्गाय नमः

He is unmanifested and perfect in His wisdom.

130. Vedanga: *With The Vedas As His Organs*

ॐ वेदाङ्गाय नमः

He has the Vedas as His Parts.

131. Vedavit: *One Who Knows All The Vedas*

ॐ वेदविदे नमः

He understands and spreads the knowledge of the Vedas.

132. Kavi: *The All-seer*

ॐ कवये नमः

He sees everything, for He is all-knowing and intelligent.

133. Lokadhyaksha: *The Lord Of The Worlds*

ॐ लोकाध्यक्षाय नमः

He witnesses the whole universe, seeing all as involved in nature.

134. Suradhyaksha: *The Lord Of The Immortals*

ॐ सुराध्यक्षाय नमः

He presides over the gods who are to be worshipped with ceremonies.

135. Dharmadhyaksha: *The Superintendent Of Dharma*

ॐ धर्माध्यक्षाय नमः

He dispenses justice according to the virtues and vices of all beings.

136. Krutakruta: *Cause And Effect*

ॐ कृताकृताय नमः

He is the effect and cause in the form of the worlds.

137. Chaturatma: *Fourfold In His Nature*

ॐ चतुरात्मने नमः

For the purpose of creation, Brahma, Time, etc., are His powers. For sustenance, Manu, Time, and all creatures are His energies. For universal Dissolution, Rudra, Time, Death, etc., are His energies.

138. Chaturvyuha: *Of Four Manifestations*

ॐ चतुर्व्यूहाय नमः

He manifests as Vasudeva, Samkarshana, Pradyumna and Aniruddha, and performs the work of creation in these forms.

139. Chaturdamshtra: *The One With Four Fangs*

ॐ चतुर्दंष्ट्राय नमः

In His incarnation as Narasimha (Man-lion), He had four fangs.

140. Chaturbhuja: *The Four-armed*

ॐ चतुर्भुजाय नमः

He is the Almighty with four arms.

141. Bhrajishnu: *The Radiant*

ॐ भ्राजिष्णवे नमः

He is pure luminosity.

142. Bhojanam: *The Object Of Enjoyment*

ॐ भोजनाय नमः

He, as Essence, is enjoyed by worshippers.

143. Bhokta: *The Experiencer*

ॐ भोक्त्रे नमः

As Purusha, he enjoys the Prakriti or Maya.

144. Sahishnu: *The Subduer*

ॐ सहिष्णवे नमः

He subdues or suppresses demons like Hiranyaksha.

145. Jagadadija: *Born Of The World-cause*

ॐ जगदादिजाय नमः

He manifests Himself as *Hiranyagarbha* or the Golden Egg at the beginning of the creation.

146. Anagha: *The Sinless*

ॐ अनघाय नमः

He is untainted by sin, in spite of residing in the midst of humanity in His incarnations.

147. Vijaya: *Excelling Everything*

ॐ विजयाय नमः

He has mastery over everything, excelling in wisdom, greatness, etc.

148. Jeta: *Transcending All Beings*

ॐ जेत्रे नमः

He is superior to all beings and naturally transcends them.

149. Vishwayoni: *The Source Of The Universe*

ॐ विश्वयोनवे नमः

He is the only cause of the universe.

150. Punarvasu: *The Repeated Dweller*

ॐ पुनर्वसवे नमः

He dwells again and again in the bodies as the Self.

151. Upendra: *The Younger Brother Of Indra*

ॐ उपेन्द्राय नमः

In His incarnation as Vamana, he was the younger brother of Indra, their parents being Aditi and Kashyapa.

152. Vamana: *The Dwarf*

ॐ वामनाय नमः

To check the pride of Bali, He came as Vamana.

153. Pramshu: *The Tall*

ॐ प्रांशवे नमः

As Vamana the dwarf, He rose to great heights, transcending all worlds, after curbing Bali's pride.

154. Amogha: *Fruitful*

ॐ अमोघाय नमः

He is always fruitful in His actions.

155. Shuchi: *The Pure*

ॐ शुचये नमः

He purifies those that worship, praise and remember Him.

156. Urjita: *The Powerful*

ॐ ऊर्जिताय नमः

He is of infinite strength.

157. Atindra: *He Who Transcends Indra*

ॐ अतीन्द्राय नमः

He is superior to Indra in all ways.

158. Samgraha: *The Withdrawer Of All*

ॐ संग्रहाय नमः

He withdraws everything unto Himself during Dissolution.

159. Sarga: *The Creation Or Creator*

ॐ सर्गाय नगः

He is the universe, or the cause of creation.

160. Dhrutatma: *Of Sustained Self*

ॐ धृतात्मने नमः

He remains changeless in His inherent form or nature.

161. Niyama: *The Director*

ॐ नियमाय नमः

He appoints beings in particular stations.

162. Yama: *The Controller*

ॐ यमाय नमः

He regulates all beings dwelling in them.

163. Vedya: *The Knowable*

ॐ वेद्याय नमः

He has to be known by aspirants seeking *moksha*.

164. Vaidya: *The Knower Of All Lores*

ॐ वैद्याय नमः

He knows all the branches of knowledge.

165. Sadayogi: *The Eternal Yogin*

ॐ सदायोगिने नमः

He is ever existent, and His essence is ever manifest.

166. Viraha: *The Slayer Of Heroic Asuras*

ॐ वीरघ्ने नमः

He slays the valiant demons for the protection of Dharma.

167. Madhava: *The Lord Of Knowledge*

ॐ माधवाय नमः

He is the Lord (*dhava*) of *ma* (knowledge).

168. Madhu: *The Honey*

ॐ मधवे नमः

Like honey, He causes great satisfaction and gives unfounded joy.

169. Atindriya: *Transcending All Senses*

ॐ अतीन्द्रियाय नमः

He is beyond all the senses.

170. Mahamaya: *The Great Illusionist*

ॐ महामायाय नमः

He can subject the greatest illusionists to illusion.

171. Mahotsaha: *Of Great Diligence*

ॐ महोत्साहाय नमः

He is ever busy in creating, sustaining and in Dissolution.

172. Mahabala: *Of Great Strength*

ॐ महाबलाय नमः

He is the strongest among the strong.

173. Mahabuddhi: *Of Mighty Intellect*

ॐ महाबुद्धये नमः

He is the wisest among the wise.

174. Mahavirya: *The Most Powerful One*

ॐ महावीर्याय नमः

His strength is never diminished.

175. Mahashakti: *Of Immense Power*

ॐ महाशक्तये नमः

His power and strength are inconceivable.

176. Mahadyuti: *Of Great Splendour*

ॐ महाद्युतये नमः

He is extremely brilliant, internally and externally.

177. Anirdeshyavapu: *Of Undefinable Form*

ॐ अनिर्देश्यवपुषे नमः

He is self-realised and cannot be defined as 'this' or 'that'.

178. Shriman: *The Lord Of All Prosperity*

ॐ श्रीमते नमः

He is endowed with greatness and prosperities.

179. Ameyatma: *Of Immeasurable Intelligence*

ॐ अमेयात्मने नमः

His intelligence cannot be measured by anyone.

180. Mahadridhruk: *Bearer Of The Great Mountain*

ॐ महाद्रिधृषे नमः

He supported the Mandara and Govardhana mountains when the ocean was churned and when the cows were protected.

181. Maheshvasa: *Of Mighty Bow*

ॐ महेष्वासाय नमः

He was ready to use the bow to protect the good.

182. Mahibharta: *The Upholder Of The Earth*

ॐ महीभर्त्रे नमः

When the earth was submerged in the great waters during Dissolution, He held it up.

183. Shrinivasa: *The Dwelling Place Of Shri*

ॐ श्रीनिवासाय नमः

Shri (Lakshmi) eternal in nature, dwells on His chest.

184. Satamgati: *The Refuge Of The Good*

ॐ सतांगतये नमः

To the followers of the Vedas, He is the means of attaining the highest destiny.

185. Aniruddha: *The Unobstructed*

ॐ अनिरुद्धाय नमः

He has never been obstructed by any from manifesting in various forms.

186. Surananda: *He Who Gladdens The Gods*

ॐ सुरानन्दाय नमः

He bestows joy on all divinities.

187. Govinda: *The Reclaimer Of The Earth*

ॐ गोविन्दाय नमः

He restored the earth that had been hidden in the depths of the ocean.

188. Govindampati: *The Lord Of The Wise*

ॐ गोविदांपतये नमः

He is the Lord of the knowers of the Vedas.

189. Marichi: *The Refulgent*

ॐ मरीचये नमः

He is the splendour of the resplendent, outshining the most brilliant.

190. Damana: *The Subduer*

ॐ दमनाय नमः

He punishes those who stray from the path of Dharma.

191. Hamsa: *The Destroyer Of Fear*

ॐ हंसाय नमः

He destroys the fear of samsara of those who meditate on Him. It also means He who moves in all bodies.

192. Suparna: *Of Beautiful Wings*

ॐ सुपर्णाय नमः

He has two beautiful wings in the form of Dharma and Adharma.

193. Bhujagottama: *The Best Of Divine Serpents*

ॐ भुजगोत्तमाय नमः

The great divine serpents, like Adisesha and Vasuki, are His powers.

194. Hiranyanabbha: *Of Golden-hued Navel*

ॐ हिरण्यनाभाय नमः

His navel is auspicious and bright like gold.

195. Sutapa: *Of Excellent Austerities*

ॐ सुतपसे नमः

He has excellent concentration of mind and senses at Badarikashrama, practising austerities as Nara and Narayana.

196. Padmanabha: *Of Lotus-shaped Navel*

ॐ पद्मनाभाय नमः

With a beautiful lotus-shaped navel, He shines in the heart-lotus of all.

197. Prajapati: *The Protector Of Beings*

ॐ प्रजापतये नमः

As Father of all beings, He protects them.

198. Amrutyu: *The Deathless*

ॐ अमृत्यवे नमः

He is without death or its cause.

199. Sarvadri: *All-seeing*

ॐ सर्वदृशे नमः

He sees the actions of all beings through His innate vision.

200. Simha: *The Destroyer Of Sins*

ॐ सिंहाय नमः

He destroys the sins of devotees when they merely remember Him.

201. Sandhata: *The Regulator*

ॐ संधात्रे नमः

He unites the beings with the fruits of their actions.

202. Sandhiman: *The Experiencer*

ॐ संधिमते नमः

He Himself experiences and enjoys the fruits of actions of the beings.

203. Sthira: *The Constant*

ॐ स्थिराय नमः

He is changeless, always remaining the same.

204. Aja: *The Mover*

ॐ अजाय नमः

He moves into the hearts of devotees. Or, He destroys the demons by throwing them.

205. Durmarshana: *The Unbearable*

ॐ दुर्मर्षणाय नमः

The demons cannot bear His might.

206. Shasta: *The Teacher*

ॐ शास्त्रे नमः

He instructs all through the scriptures.

207. Vishrutatma: *Of Renowned Self*

ॐ विश्रुतात्मने नमः

He is specially glorified and known through terms like truth, wisdom, knowledge, etc.

208. Surariha: *The Destroyer Of Enemies*

ॐ सुरारिघ्ने नमः

He destroys the foes of gods.

209. Guru: *The Preceptor*

ॐ गुरवे नमः

He is the supreme Preceptor of all knowledge.

210. Gurutama: *The Supreme Teacher*

ॐ गुरुतमाय नमः

He imparts brahmavidya or knowledge of Brahman to divinities like Brahma.

211. Dhama: *The Effulgence*

ॐ धाम्ने नमः

He is the supreme Light or the ultimate support of all values.

212. Satya: *Truth*

ॐ सत्यायै नमः

He is the essence of truth, hence Truth is said to be supreme.

213. Satyaparakrama: *Of Unfailing Valour*

ॐ सत्यपराक्रमाय नमः

He is of unfailing valour.

214. Nimisha: *With Eyes Closed*

ॐ निमिषाय नमः

His eyes are closed in *Yoganidra* (yogic sleep).

215. Animisha: *The Ever-Wakeful*

ॐ अनिमिषाय नमः

He is ever awake; in His matsya (fish) incarnation, he has no eyelids and hence always awake. He is the Self ever awake.

216. Sragvi: *The Garlanded One*

ॐ स्रग्विणे नमः

He always wears the garland called the Vaijayanti, which is strung with the subtle aspects of the elements.

217. Vachaspati Udaradhi: *The Lord Of Knowledge*

ॐ वाचस्पतये उदारधिये नमः

He is the Master of *Vak* or Word (knowledge) being of brilliant intelligence.

218. Agrani: *Leader To The Highest Status*

ॐ अग्रण्ये नमः

He leads all liberation seekers to the supreme status.

219. Gramani: *The Director Of The Group*

ॐ ग्रामण्ये नमः

He directs the assembly of beings in all activities.

220. Shriman: *The Radiant*

ॐ श्रीमते नमः

He is the resplendent Light which excels all.

221. Nyaya: *The Argument*

ॐ न्यायाय नमः

He is the argument which enunciates distinction and sustains proof.

222. Neta: *The Regulator*

ॐ नेत्रे नमः

He regulates the functioning of the cosmos.

223. Samirana: *The Breath*

ॐ समीरणाय नमः

He is the Breath which keeps all beings functioning.

224. Sahasramurdha: *The Thousand-headed*

ॐ सहस्रमूर्ध्ने नमः

He has a thousand or innumerable heads.

30

225. Vishwatma: *The Universal Self*

ॐ विश्वात्मने नमः

He is the Soul of the universe, manifesting Himself by His knowledge.

226. Sahasraksha: *The Thousand-eyed*

ॐ सहस्राक्षाय नमः

He has innumerable eyes.

227. Sahasrapat: *The Thousand-footed*

ॐ सहस्रपदे नमः

He has innumerable legs.

228. Avartana: *The Spinner Of The Wheel Of Samsara*

ॐ आवर्तनाय नमः

He turns or spins the wheel of worldly life.

229. Nivruttatma: *The Unbound Self*

ॐ निवृत्तात्मने नमः

He is free from the bonds of worldly life.

230. Samvruta: *He Who Is Veiled*

ॐ संवृताय नमः

He is veiled by *avidya* (nescience or ignorance) that covers Him.

231. Sampramardana: *The Crusher*

ॐ संप्रमर्दनाय नमः

He manifests as Rudra, Yama, etc., to destroy beings.

232. Ahahsamvartaka: *The Regulator Of Day*

ॐ अहः संवर्तकाय नमः

He regulates the day, the time, etc.

233. Vahni: *The Fire*

ॐ वह्नवे नमः

As Fire, He carries the oblations made to the gods in sacrifices.

234. Anila: *The Beginningless*

ॐ अनिलाय नमः

He is without any beginning. Or, He moves as He has no fixed residence. Or, He is unaffected by virtue and vice.

235. Dharanidhara: *The Bearer Of The Earth*

ॐ धरणीधराय नमः

As Adisesha and Vamana He supports the world.

236. Suprasada: *The Gracious*

ॐ सुप्रसादाय नमः

He is gracious to wrong-doers like Shishupala, and gives them salvation.

237. Prasannatma: *Of Delightful Nature*

ॐ प्रसन्नात्मने नमः

His inner sense remains uncontaminated by rajas (passion) or tamas (inertia). Or, He is extremely merciful. Or, He is self-satisfied.

238. Vishwadhruk: *The Overlord Of The Cosmos*

ॐ विश्वधृषे नमः

He holds the universe by His power.

239. Vishwabhuk: *The Enjoyer Of The Universe*

ॐ विश्वभुजे नमः

He enjoys and protects the universe.

240. Vibhu: *The Multiformed*

ॐ विभवे नमः

He is multiformed, such as Hiranyagarbha, and is eternal.

241. Satkarta: *One Who Offers Benefits*

ॐ सत्कर्त्रे नमः

He honours the good by offering them benefits.

242. Satkruta: *The Worshipful*

ॐ सत्कृताय नमः

He is worshipped by even those who deserve to be worshipped.

243. Sadhu: *The Righteous*

ॐ साधवे नमः

He acts according to justice. Or, He achieves everything. Or, He is the material cause for everything.

244. Jahnu: *The Disintegrator*

ॐ जह्नवे नमः

He dissolves all beings during the withdrawal of the universe. Or, He leads the devotees to salvation.

245. Narayana: *The Abode Of All During Pralaya*

ॐ नारायणाय नमः

He has His residence in all beings, and at the time of Dissolution, He is their abode.

246. Nara: *The Leader*

ॐ नराय नमः

He is the eternal *Paramatma* as He leads.

247. Asankhyeya: *The Unaccountable*

ॐ असंख्येयाय नमः

He is without attributes, and no form, number, name can be attached to Him.

248. Aprameyatma: *The Immeasurable Self*

ॐ अप्रमेयात्मने नमः

His nature cannot be assessed by any means of knowledge.

249. Vishishta: *The Transcendental*

ॐ विशिष्टाय नमः

He transcends and excels all.

33

250. Shishtakrut: *The Commander*

ॐ शिष्टकृते नमः

He commands everything. Or, He protects the good.

251. Shuchi: *The Pure*

ॐ शुचये नमः

He is stainless, free of any impurity.

252. Siddhartha: *One Whose Objects Are Fulfilled*

ॐ सिद्धार्थाय नमः

He gets whatever He desires.

253. Siddhasankalpa: *Of Accomplished Resolutions*

ॐ सिद्धसंकल्पाय नमः

His resolutions are always fulfilled.

254. Siddhidah: *The Bestower Of Fruits*

ॐ सिद्धिदाय नमः

He bestows fulfilment on those who practise discipline.

255. Siddhisadhana: *The Promoter Of Achievements*

ॐ सिद्धिसाधनाय नमः

He brings fulfilment to actions or work that deserve it.

256. Vrushahi: *The Revealer Of Dharma*

ॐ वृषाहिणे नमः

He reveals the paths of righteousness or Dharma.

257. Vrushabha: *The Showerer Of Desired Objects*

ॐ वृषभाय नमः

He showers on His devotees all that they pray for.

258. Vishnu: *The Pervader*

ॐ विष्णवे नमः

He pervades everything, transversing this universe by three steps.

259. Vrushaparva: *Having Dharma As Steps*

ॐ वृषपर्वणे नमः

Those who want to attain the supreme state must tread the path of Dharma.

260. Vrushodara: *In Whom All Beings Are Contained*

ॐ वृषोदराय नमः

He is the source of all beings.

261. Vardhana: *The Nourisher*

ॐ वर्धनाय नमः

He nourishes and augments the needs of His devotees.

262. Vardhamana: *One Who Expands*

ॐ वर्धमानाय नमः

He expands in the form of the universe, enriching His people in every respect.

263. Vivikta: *The Solitary*

ॐ विविक्ताय नमः

He is unaffected and untouched by anything, being unattached.

264. Shrutisagara: *The Ocean Of Scriptures*

ॐ श्रुतिसागराय नमः

Through Him flow the *shruti* or Ve ': words.

265. Subhuja: *Of Excellent Arms*

ॐ सुभुजाय नमः

He has majestic arms that protect the world.

266. Durdhara: *Difficult To Be Borne*

ॐ दुर्धराय नमः

He holds up the earth which holds all. Or, He cannot be held by anyone. Or, Those who seek salvation find it difficult to hold Him in mind while meditating.

267. Vagmi: *From Whom Sacred Speech Emanates*

ॐ वाग्मिने नमः

The Vedic words pour from Him.

268. Mahendra: *The Lord Of Lords*

ॐ महेन्द्राय नमः

He is the supreme Being, the Lord of all lords.

269. Vasuda: *The Bestower Of Wealth*

ॐ वसुदाय नमः

He is the consumer of food and giver of wealth.

270. Vasu: *Wealth*

ॐ वसवे नमः

The wealth which He gives to others is Himself. Or, He veils Himself in maya. Or, He lives in space alone.

271. Naikarupa: *Of Many Forms*

ॐ नैकरुपाय नमः

By His maya, He appears in many forms.

272. Bruhadrupa: *Of Immense Form*

ॐ बृहद्रूपाय नमः

He has manifested in immense forms, for example, Varaha, the boar.

273. Shipivishtta: *The Self Of Sacrificial Animals*

ॐ शिपिविष्टाय नमः

He resides in the sacrificial animals in the form or *yajna* or sacrifice. Or, He is the Lord of the cosmos residing in the rays.

274. Prakashana: *The Illuminator*

ॐ प्रकाशनाय नमः

He illumines everything and reveals His form to His devotees.

275. Ojas-tejo-dyutidhara: *The Possessor Of Virtuous Qualities*

ॐ ओजस्तेजोद्युतिधराय नमः

He possesses life-energy, valour and effulgence, having the radiance of knowledge too.

276. Prakashatma: *The Radiant Self*

ॐ प्रकाशात्मने नमः

His radiant form and supreme nature can be known through devotion.

277. Pratapana: *The Energiser*

ॐ प्रतापनाय नमः

By His manifestations as the sun, He energises the world.

278. Riddha: *Wealthy*

ॐ ऋद्धाय नमः

He is wealthy in excellences like Dharma, knowledge, dispassion, etc.

279. Spashtakshara: *Of Clear Verbalisation*

ॐ स्पष्टाक्षराय नमः

He is the syllable Om, whose sound is acute.

280. Mantra: *The Sacred Formula*

ॐ मन्त्राय नमः

He is *Rig, Yajus* and *Saman* (the Vedas). Or, He is known or revealed in the mantras.

281. Chandramshu: *The Ray of the Moon*

ॐ चन्द्रांशवे नमः

Like the rays of the moon, He brings delight to those affected by the scorching rays of samsara (worldly life).

282. Bhaskaradyuti: *Bright As The Sun*

ॐ भास्करद्युतये नमः

He is as bright as the brilliant light of the sun.

283. Amritamshoodbhava: *The Source of the Moon*

ॐ अमृतांशूद्भवाय नमः

He is the source from whom the moon originated at the time of the churning of the milky ocean.

284. Bhanu: *The Radiant*

ॐ भानवे नमः

When He shines, everything else shines, and the sun depends on Him.

285. Shashabindu: *The Moon*

ॐ शशबिन्दवे नमः

Like the moon, He nourishes all beings.

286. Sureshwara: *Lord Of The Gods*

ॐ सुरेश्वराय नमः

He is the Lord of the gods and the munificent donors.

287. Aushadham: *The Medicine*

ॐ औषधाय नमः

He is the Medicine for the miseries of the world.

288. Jagata Setu: *The Bridge Of The World*

ॐ जगतः सेतवे नमः

He is the Bridge for crossing the ocean of worldly life. Or, Like a bridge he preserves the social order.

289. Satyadharmaparakrama: *Of True Dharma and Prowess*

ॐ सत्यधर्मपराक्रमाय नमः

His virtues like Dharma and knowledge are unfailing.

290. Bhutabhavyabhavannatha: *The Lord Of The Beings Of Past, Present And Future*

ॐ भूतभव्यभवन्नाथाय नमः

All beings seek Him. Or, He disciplines all beings. Or, He blesses all beings. Or, He rules them.

291. Pavana: *The Purifier*

ॐ पवनाय नमः

He is the wind among the purifiers.

292. Paavana: *One Who Causes Movement*

ॐ पावनाय नमः

He causes movement and in obedience to Him, the wind blows.

293. Anala: *One Who Embodies The Vital Breaths*

ॐ अनलाय नमः

The beings receive the vital breaths as their Self. Or, He is beyond smell. Or, For Him, nothing is limited.

294. Kamaha: *The Destroyer of Desire*

ॐ कामघ्ने नमः

He destroys the desire of those who seek salvation. Or, He destroys the evil intents of His devotees, enemies.

295. Kamakrut: *The Fulfiller of Desires*

ॐ कामकृते नमः

He fulfils the desires of pure-minded devotees. Or, He is the Father of Kama (Pradyumna) in His incarnation as Krishna.

296. Kanta: *The Beautiful*

ॐ कान्ताय नमः

He is the most beautiful.

297. Kama: *The Desired*

ॐ कामाय नमः

He is desired by those who seek the four supreme values of life.

298. Kamaprada: *The Granter of All Desires*

ॐ कामप्रदाय नमः

He liberally fulfils the desires of His devotees.

299. Prabhu: *The Really Existent*

ॐ प्रभवे नमः

He surpasses all, and specially attracts the eyes and mind of all by His beauty.

300. Yugadikrut: *The Creator Of Ages*

ॐ युगादिकृते नमः

He instituted the yugas or ages of the world.

301. Yugavarta: *The Cause Of The Cycle Of Ages*

ॐ युगावर्ताय नमः

Being Time, He brings about the cycle of yugas.

302. Naikamaya: *Of Many Illusions*

ॐ नैकमायाय नमः

He assumes many forms of maya.

303. Mahashana: *Consumer Of Everything*

ॐ महाशनाय नमः

He is one who absorbs everything at the end of dissolution.

304. Adrushya: *The Invisible*

ॐ अदृश्याय नमः

He is beyond the intellect and senses.

305. Vyaktarupa: *Of Manifested Forms*

ॐ व्यक्तरूपाय नमः

He can be perceived in His manifested form. Or being self-luminous, He is clearly perceived by the sages.

306. Sahasrajit: *The Conqueror Of Thousands*

ॐ सहस्रजिते नमः

He is victorious over the demons in battle.

307. Anantajit: *The Conqueror Of Innumerable Beings*

ॐ अनन्तजिते नमः

He is victorious over all beings at all times.

308. Ishtta: *The Beloved*

ॐ इष्टाय नमः

He is dear to all for He is supreme Bliss, Or, He is worshipped in the sacrifices.

309. Avishishtta: *Non-specialised*

ॐ अविशिष्टाय नमः

As the Non-specialised, He dwells in all.

310. Shishteshta: *Loved By The Scholars*

ॐ शिष्टेष्टाय नमः

He is dear to the learned. Or, He loves the learned.

311. Shikhandi: *Decorated With Peacock-feathers*

ॐ शिरवण्डिने नमः

As Krishna, He uses peacock feathers for His crown.

312. Nahusha: *The Confounder*

ॐ नहुषाय नमः

He confounds every being with His illusive powers or maya.

313. Vrusha: *In The Form Of Dharma*

ॐ वृषाय नमः

He is Dharma, for He showers all desires.

314. Krodhaha: *The Destroyer Of Anger*

ॐ त्रोधघ्ने नमः

He destroys anger in the virtuous.

315. Krodhakrutkarta: *The Creator Of Anger*

ॐ त्रोधकृत्कर्त्रे नमः

He generates anger in the evil. Or, He is the creator of the universe. Or, He is the slayer of the evil.

316. Vishwabahu: *With Arms On All Sides*

ॐ विश्वबाहवे नमः

He has arms everywhere. Or, He is the support of all.

317. Mahidhara: *The Bearer Of The Earth*

ॐ महीधराय नमः

He supports the earth. Or, He receives all forms of worship.

318. Achyuta: *Unlapsing From His Nature*

ॐ अच्युताय नमः

He is free from the six changes, like birth, death, etc., and is eternal.

319. Prathita: *The Renowned*

ॐ प्रथिताय नमः

He is renowned due to His creation, etc., of the universe.

320. Prana: *The Life*

ॐ प्राणाय नमः

He is the life-force of all beings.

321. Pranada: *The Life-giver*

ॐ प्राणदाय नमः

He gives Life to the gods and also destroys the life of demons.

322. Vasavanuja: *The Younger Brother Of Indra*

ॐ वासवानुजाय नमः

He was born to Kashyapa and Aditi, as was Indra.

323. Apamnidhi: *The Ocean*

ॐ अपांनिधये नमः

Among all pools of water, He is the Ocean.

324. Adhishttanam: *The Mainstay*

ॐ अधिष्ठानाय नमः

He, as the material cause of everything, is their substance and support.

325. Apramatta: *The Vigilant*

ॐ अप्रमत्ताय नमः

He is always vigilant in awarding the fruits of action to the recipients.

42

326. Pratishttita: *The Well-established*

ॐ प्रतिष्ठिताय नमः

He is well-established in His own glory.

327. Skanda: *One Who Flows*

ॐ स्कन्दाय नमः

He flows as nectar. Or, He dries up everything like the wind does.

328. Skandadhara: *The Supporter Of The Righteous Path*

ॐ स्कन्दधराय नमः

He incarnates Himself to uphold the righteous path.

329. Dhurya: *The Bearer Of The Yoke*

ॐ धुर्याय नमः

He bears the weight of the burden of all beings in the form of birth, etc.

330. Varada: *The Granter of Boons*

ॐ वरदाय नमः

He grants boons or desired objects. Or, Himself being the Sacrifice, He distributes the sacrificial fee in sacrifices.

331. Vayuvahana: *The Director Of The Vital Air*

ॐ वायुवाहनाय नमः

He vibrates the seven *Vayus* or atmospheres, beginning with *Avaha*.

332. Vasudeva: *The Indwelling Player*

ॐ वासुदेवाय नमः

Like the sun with its rays, He covers the whole universe, and resides in all beings.

333. Bruhadbhanu: *The Great Brilliance*

ॐ बृहद्भानवे नमः

He illumines the whole world with the rays which surpass the sun, moon and others.

334. Adideva: *The First Deity*

ॐ आदिदेवाय नमः

He is the Divinity who is the source of all gods (devas).

335. Purandara: *The Destroyer of Cities*

ॐ पुरन्दराय नमः

He destroys the cities of the enemies of the gods.

336. Ashoka: *The Unafflicted*

ॐ अशोकाय नमः

He is free from sorrow, infatuation, thirst, hunger, birth, and death.

337. Tarana: *The Uplifter From Samsara*

ॐ तारणाय नमः

He enables one to cross the samsara (worldly life).

338. Tara: *The Saviour*

ॐ ताराय नमः

He liberates beings from fears attending birth, old age and death.

339. Shura: *The Valiant*

ॐ शूराय नमः

He, being of great prowess, fulfils the four paths of life—dharma, artha, kama and moksha.

340. Shauri: *The Descendant Of Shura*

ॐ शौराये नमः

In His incarnation as Krishna, He was a grandson of Shura.

341. Janeshwar: *Lord Of Men*

ॐ जनेश्वराय नमः

He is the Lord of all beings.

342. Anukula: *The Favourable To All*

ॐ अनुकूलाय नमः

Being the Self of all, He is favourable to all, for none does anything which is unfavourable to himself.

44

343. Shatavarta: *One Who Incarnates Several Times*

ॐ शतावर्ताय नमः

He takes several incarnations to set the world right. Or. He, as life-force, flows through various nerves.

344. Padmi: *With Lotus In Hand*

ॐ पद्मिने नमः

He is always seen with a lotus in His hand.

345. Padmanibhekshana: *With Eyes Like Lotus*

ॐ पद्मनिभेक्षणाय नमः

His eyes resembles the lotus.

346. Padmanabha: *Seated In The Lotus Centre*

ॐ पद्मनाभाय नमः

He resides or is seated in the pericarp of the lotus (of the universe).

347. Aravindaksha: *Lotus-eyed*

ॐ अरविन्दाक्षाय नमः

His eyes resemble the lotus.

348. Padmagarbha: *Contained In The Lotus*

ॐ पद्मगर्भाय नमः

He is meditated upon in the centre of the lotus of the heart.

349. Sharirabhrut: *Nourisher Of Bodies*

ॐ शरीरभृते नमः

He nourishes beings through food and life-energy. Or, He supports them through His maya.

350. Mahardhi: *Supremely Splendid*

ॐ महर्द्धये नमः

He has no end to His divine powers.

351. Riddha: *The Expanse*

ॐ ऋद्धाय नमः

He is the expanse in the form of the universe.

352. Vruddhatma: *The Ancient Self*

ॐ वृद्धात्मने नमः

His body is *vriddha* or ancient.

353. Mahaksha: *The Great-eyed*

ॐ महाक्षाय नमः

He has two or many glorious eyes. Or, He possesses divine senses unattached to objects.

354. Garudadhwaja: *Having Garuda As His Emblem*

ॐ गरूडध्वजाय नमः

The Garuda adorns His flag as an emblem, besides being His vehicle.

355. Atula: *The Incomparable*

ॐ अतुलाय नमः

No one is as great as or superior to Him.

356. Sharabha: *The Inner Self*

ॐ शरभाय नमः

He shines in bodies as the individual Self.

357. Bhima: *The Awe-inspiring*

ॐ भीमाय नमः

He is the One whom all fear. Or, He causes no fear to those who tread the righteous path.

358. Samayajna: *The Knower Of The Doctrines*

ॐ समयज्ञाय नमः

He is well-versed in the art of creation and preservation of the world. Or, To Him, worship consists in the attitude of equality towards all.

359. Havirhari: *The Receiver Of Oblations*

ॐ हविर्हरये नमः

He is the enjoyer and also the Lord of all sacrifices. Or, He is worshipped through oblations. Or, He removes nescience and its effect on worldly life. Or, He is so called on account of His blue complexion. Or, He destroys the sins of the men on their merely remembering Him.

360. Sarvalakshanalakshanya: *Known Through All Methods Of Research*

ॐ सर्वलक्षणलक्षण्याय नमः

He is the One Supreme Reality as all methods of proof disclose.

361. Lakshmivan: *The Consort Of Lakshmi*

ॐ लक्ष्मीवते नमः

Lakshmi, His consort and the goddess of prosperity, ever resides on His chest.

362. Samatinjaya: *Victorious In Battle*

ॐ समितिंजयाय नमः

He is always victorious in fights, and destroys pains of the devotees.

363. Vikshara: *Undecaying*

ॐ विक्षराय नमः

He is without any form of destruction.

364. Rohita: *The Red-hued*

ॐ रोहिताय नमः

He assumes a red-hued form at will. Or, He took the incarnation of a fish (Mastsya).

365. Marga: *The Path*

ॐ मार्गाय नमः

He is sought after by those who desire liberation. Or, He is the path to supreme bliss.

47

366. Hetu: *The Cause*

ॐ हेतवे नमः

He is the material and instrumental cause of the universe.

367. Damodara: *Known Through Discipline*

ॐ दामोदराय नमः

He is known through the mind which is purified by self-control of the senses. Or, As Krishna, He was tied by a cord round His waist to two trees (dama= cord, and udara= waist). Or, Dama means the worlds, and in His abdomen these worlds have their existence.

368. Saha: *All-enduring*

ॐ सहाय नमः

He forgives the wrongs of His devotees. Or, He supersedes all.

369. Mahidhara: *The Bearer Of The Earth*

ॐ महीधराय नमः

He props up the earth in the shape of mountains.

370. Mahabhaga: *The Most Fortunate*

ॐ महाभागाय नमः

He is very fortunate in taking His incarnations. Or, He takes a body by His own will. He enjoys supreme felicities.

371. Vegavan: *The Swift*

ॐ वेगवते नमः

He is swifter than the mind.

372. Amitashana: *Of Unmeasured Appetite*

ॐ अमिताशना नमः

He consumes the worlds during Dissolution.

373. Udbhava: *The Origin*

ॐ उद्भवाय नमः

He is the material cause of the universe. Or, He is free from transmigratory existence.

374. Kshobhana: *The Agitator*

ॐ क्षोभणाय नमः

At the time of creation, He agitates at His will the perishable Prakriti and the imperishable Purusha.

375. Deva: *The Deity*

ॐ देवाय नमः

He conquers the enemies of gods, dwells in all beings, shines as the universal Self, is praised by holy men, and pervades all — there is only One God.

376. Shrigarbha: *Containing Shri In Himself*

ॐ श्रीगर्भाय नमः

Shri or glory is within Him in the form of the universe.

377. Parameshwara: *The Supreme Lord*

ॐ परमेश्वराय नमः

He remains alike in all beings.

378. Karanam: *The Instrument*

ॐ करणाय नमः

He is the cause in the creation of the universe.

379. Kaaranam: *The Material Cause*

ॐ कारणाय नमः

He is both the instrumental and the material cause of creation.

380. Karta: *The Doer*

ॐ कर्त्रे नमः

He is free and independent, and is therefore His own Master.

381. Vikarta: *The Creator Of The Various Worlds*

ॐ विकर्त्रे नमः

He is the creator of this unique universe, as also many others.

382. Gahana: *The Unknowable*

ॐ गहनाय नमः

He is the supreme Almighty whose nature, greatness and actions cannot be known by anybody.

383. Guha: *The Concealer*

ॐ गुहाय नमः

He hides His nature, etc. by His power of Maya.

384. Vyavasaya: *Determination*

ॐ व्यवसायाय नमः

Being the Creator of the intellect, He is pure wisdom.

385. Vyavasthana: *The Basis*

ॐ व्यवस्थानाय नमः

As the basis of everything, He regulates the guardians of the universe and their respective functions; and also all life, and the four stages of life.

386. Samsthana: *The Ultimate Abode*

ॐ संस्थानाय नमः

In Him dwell all beings during Dissolution, Or He is the supreme goal.

387. Sthanada: *The Conferer Of Status*

ॐ स्थानदाय नमः

He confers particular status on Dhruva (Pole Star) and the rest according to their actions or deeds.

388. Dhruva: *The Firm*

ॐ ध्रुवाय नमः

He is indestructible, for He is eternal.

389. Parardhi: *The Supreme Manifestation*

ॐ परर्द्धये नमः

He possesses lordliness of the most exalted type.

50

390. Paramaspashta: *Completely Evident*

ॐ परमस्पष्टाय नमः

He is evident on account of showing His grace to all.

391. Tushta: *The Contented*

ॐ तुष्टाय नमः

He is contented since He is the supreme Bliss.

392. Pushta: *The Plenary*

ॐ पुष्टाय नमः

He is full on account of His qualities.

393. Shubhekshana: *Of Auspicious Mien*

ॐ शुभेक्षणाय नमः

His vision bestows good on all beings.

394. Rama: *The Felicitous*

ॐ रामाय नमः

He is the eternally blissful, One in whom the yogis find delight.

395. Virama: *The Goal*

ॐ विरामाय नमः

All beings seek Him as the goal.

396. Virata: *Passionless.*

ॐ विरताय नमः

He is not attached to enjoyments of objects.

397. Marga: *The Way*

ॐ मार्गाय नमः

He is the Path, knowing whom the liberation-seeking aspirants attain immortality.

398. Neya: *The Conducted*

ॐ नेयाय नमः

He is the One who directs the beings to the supreme Being through spiritual realisation.

399. Naya: *The Leader*

ॐ नयाय नमः

He is the Leader in the form of spiritual illumination, and conceived in three Ways — the Way, the Conducted, and the Leader.

400. Anaya: *Not Conducted By Anyone*

ॐ अनयाय नमः

He is One whom none can lead.

401. Vira: *The Valiant*

ॐ वीराय नमः

He creates fear in the lesser beings.

402. Shaktimatam Shreshtta: *The Chief Of The Energetic*

ॐ शक्तिमतां श्रेष्ठाय नमः

He excels everyone including Brahma.

403. Dharma: *The Support*

ॐ धर्माय नमः

He supports all beings. Or, He is adored by all dharmas.

404. Dharmaviduttama: *The Best Of The Knowers Of Dharma*

ॐ धर्मविदुत्तमाय नमः

The scriptures consisting of *shrutis* and *smritis* form His commandments, and He is the best of the knowers like Manu and Yajnavalkya.

405. Vaikuntta: *The Saviour*

ॐ वैकुण्ठाय नमः

He saves men from straying into wrong paths.

406. Purusha: *The Person*

ॐ पुरूषाय नमः

He is the One who existed before anything. Or, He is the One who can efface all sins. Or, He is the one who resides in the body.

407. Prana: *Life*

ॐ प्राणाय नमः

He lives in the form of life-giving force called Prana.

408. Pranada: *The Withdrawer of Prana*

ॐ प्राणदाय नमः

At the time of Dissolution, He withdraws life. Or, He gives life to all beings.

409. Pranava: *Praise Or Salutation*

ॐ प्रणवाय नमः

He is One who is praised by the worshipper by Om, or He who is saluted.

410. Pruthu: *The Immense*

ॐ पृथवे नमः

He expands and assumes the form of the universe.

411. Hiranyagarbha: *The Cause Of The Golden Egg*

ॐ हिरण्यगर्भाय नमः

It was from His vitality that sprang the golden Egg, the birthplace of Brahma.

412. Shatrughna: *The Destroyer Of Gods' Enemies*

ॐ शत्रुघ्राय नमः

He destroys the enemies of the gods.

413. Vyapta: *The Pervader*

ॐ व्याप्ताय नमः

He, as the cause, pervades all effects.

414. Vayu: *The Water Of Fragrance*

ॐ वायवे नमः

As the purifying smell in the earth, He Himself approaches all places irrespectively.

415. Adhokshaja: *Whose Power Does Not Diminish*

ॐ अधोक्षजाय नमः

At no time does He get diminished. Or, He manifests as the cosmic Being between Heaven and Earth. Or, When the sense organs take a course to the inner Self, the knowledge of the Lord arises.

416. Ritu: *Season In His Aspect As Time*

ॐ ऋतवे नमः

In His aspect as Kala or Time he removes the difficulties of the people by timely seasons.

417. Sudarshana: *Of Good Vision*

ॐ सुदर्शनाय नमः

His vision, that is, knowledge, leads to salvation, Or, His eyes are long and pure as the petals of the lotus. Or, He is easily seen by devotees.

418. Kala: *The Reckoner (Time)*

ॐ कालाय नमः

He, being Time among measurers, measures and sets a limit to everything.

419. Parameshtti: *Centred In His Glory*

ॐ परमेष्ठिने नमः

He dwells in His supreme Glory in the ether of the heart.

420. Parigraha: *The Receiver*

ॐ परिग्रहाय नमः

He, being everywhere, is approached on all sides by his devotees. Or, He receives the offering made by devotees.

421. Ugra: *The Formidable*

ॐ उग्राय नमः

He is the source of fear even to the sun, etc. In obedience to Him, the wind blows and the sun rises.

422. Samvatsara: *The Abode*

ॐ संवत्सराय नमः

He is the abode in whom all beings dwell.

423. Daksha: *The Efficient*

ॐ दक्षाय नमः

He manifests Himself as the universe. Or, He accomplishes everything quickly and dexterously.

424. Vishrama: *Tranquillity*

ॐ विश्रामाय नमः

He bestows liberation to aspirants beset with miseries arising from ignorance, pride, etc., and who seek relief from samsara.

425. Vishwadakshina: *The Most Skilful*

ॐ विश्वदक्षिणाय नमः

He excels others in His skill. Or, He is proficient in everything.

426. Vistara: *The Expanse*

ॐ विस्ताराय नमः

He expands in Himself all the worlds.

427. Sthavarasthanu: *The Firm And Motionless*

ॐ स्थावरास्थाणवे नमः

Long-lasting entities and apparently motionless objects like the earth rest in Him.

428. Pramanam: *The Proof*

ॐ प्रमाणाय नमः

He is pure Consciousness and authority for all dharmas.

429. Bijayavyayam: *Undecaying Seed*

ॐ बीजायाव्ययाय नमः

He is the immutable cause of samsara without Himself changing.

430. Artha: *Desired By All*

ॐ अर्थाय नमः

He is desired by all as He is Bliss.

431. Anartha: *Having No Ends*

ॐ अनर्थाय नमः

Since His desires are all fulfilled, He has no ends to seek.

432. Mahakosha: *Possessed Of Great Sheaths*

ॐ महाकोशाय नमः

His treasures, consisting of divine treasures like shankha, padma, etc., are immeasurable.

433. Mahabhoga: *Enjoying Great Bliss*

ॐ महाभोगाय नमः

Being the source of great Bliss, He enjoys it.

434. Mahadhana: *Of Great Wealth*

ॐ महाधनाय नमः

Since He is the means of attaining great happiness, devotees seek this great wealth from Him.

435. Anirvinna: *Not Depressed*

ॐ अनिर्विण्णाय नमः

Since His desires are ever-fulfilled, He is never depressed.

436. Sthavishttha: *The Most Massive*

ॐ स्थविष्ठाय नमः

As the cosmic Being, He has the fire as His head, and the sun and moon as His eyes.

437. Abhu: *The Unborn*

ॐ अभुवे नमः

He is without birth. Or He has existence.

438. Dharmayupa: *The Sacrificial Post For Dharmas*

ॐ धर्मयूपाय नमः

Like the animals for sacrifice are bound to the sacrificial post, so is He, the resting place for all dharmas which are the means of worshipping Him.

439. Mahamakha: *The Great Sacrificer*

ॐ महामखाय नमः

He is the great Sacrificer because the sacrifices offered to him confer salvation.

440. Nakshatranemi: *Nave Of The Stars*

ॐ नक्षत्रनेमये नमः

All planets, sun, moon etc., are tied to Dhruva by the bonds of Vayus forming the tail of Dhruva or Shimshumara chakra, and in the heart of this chakra is Vishnu, like a nave, regulating the whole.

441. Nakshatri: *The Lord Of Stars*

ॐ नक्षत्रिणे नमः

Among the moon, sun, etc., who are the leader of the universe, He is their leader.

442. Kshama: *The Competent*

ॐ क्षमाय नमः

He is clever and adept in all His actions. Or, He is full of patience.

443. Kshaama: *The Remainder*

ॐ क्षामाय नमः

He alone remains as the pure Self, when all else have disappeared during Dissolution.

444. Samihana: *Well-desiring*

ॐ समीहनाय नमः

He wishes all beings well and exerts for creation, etc.

445. Yajna: *Sacrifice*

ॐ यज्ञाय नमः

All the Vedic sacrifices are His powers. He gives joy to all gods in the form of *yajna*.

446. Ijya: *The Object Of Sacrifice*

ॐ इज्याय नमः

He is the object fit to be worshipped in sacrifices.

447. Mahejya: *The Great Object Of Sacrifice*

ॐ महेज्याय नमः

Of all the deities worshipped, He alone is capable of giving liberation.

448. Kratu: *The Sacrificial Ceremony*

ॐ क्रतवे नमः

The Lord is called so as He is the form of sacrifices in which there is a sacrificial post.

449. Satram: *The Expanded Sacrifice*

ॐ सत्राय नमः

He is of the nature of ordained Dharma, and the sacrifice is performed with the sacrificial post. Or, He protects the good.

450. Satamgati: *The Refuge Of The Good*

ॐ सतां गतये नमः

He is the sole refuge for those that seek salvation.

451. Sarvadarshi: *All-seeing*

ॐ सर्वदर्शिने नमः

Through His natural wisdom and insight, He perceives the good and bad actions of all.

452. Vimuktatma: *The Free Self*

ॐ विमुक्तात्मने नमः

He is naturally free. Or, Himself free, He liberates others.

453. Sarvajna: *He Is All, The Knower*

ॐ सर्वज्ञाय नमः

He recognises all as His manifestation, for He is All and the knower of all.

454. Jnanamuttamam: *Supreme Knowledge*

ॐ ज्ञानायोत्तमाय नमः

Divine knowledge, birthless and limitless, accomplishes everything.

455. Suvrata: *Of Wonderful Vow*

ॐ सुव्रताय नमः

He offers protection from all beings to one who seeks refuge in Him by even once saying "I am Thine."

456. Sumukha: *Of Beautiful Face*

ॐ सुमुखाय नमः

He is One with a pleasing, handsome and calm face, and large, beautiful eyes, wide like a lotus petal.

457. Sukshma: *The Subtle*

ॐ सूक्ष्माय नमः

He is subtle as He is free from gross causes like sound, etc.

458. Sughosha: *Of Auspicious Sound*

ॐ सुघोषाय नमः

His auspicious sound is in the form of the Vedas. Or, He has the deep and sonorous sound as that of the cloud.

459. Sukhada: *The Bestower Of Happiness*

ॐ सुखदाय नमः

He confers happiness on the righteous ones. Or, He destroys the happiness of the wicked.

460. Suhrut: *Friend*

ॐ सुह्रदे नमः

He confers benefits without seeking anything in return.

59

461. Manohara: *The Mind-captivater*

ॐ मनोहराय नमः

He captivates the mind as He is pure Bliss.

462. Jitakrodha: *The Conqueror Of Anger*

ॐ जितक्रधाय नमः

He destroys the foes of the gods, not out of anger, but in order to establish and protect righteousness.

463. Virabahu: *The Valiant- armed*

ॐ वीरबाहवे नमः

His arms are capable of heroic deeds like slaying the foes and establishing Dharma.

464. Vidarana: *The Destroyer*

ॐ विदारणाय नमः

He destroys those who live contrary to Dharma.

465. Swapana: *Stupefying*

ॐ स्वापनाय नमः

Through maya, he causes confusion to those who lose their virtues.

466. Swavasha: *The Independent*

ॐ स्ववशाय नमः

He is independent, being the sole cause of the whole cosmic process.

467. Vyapi: *All-pervading*

ॐ व्यापिने नमः

Like ether, He pervades everywhere, and is eternal. Or, as cause, He pervades all effects.

468. Naikatma: *Multiform*

ॐ नैकात्मने नमः

He manifests in different forms through His instrumental energies, during creation and rest.

469. Naikakarmakrut: *Performing Many Actions*

ॐ नैककर्मकृते नमः

He engages in innumerable activities in the process of creation, preservation and withdrawal.

470. Vatsara: *The Abode Of All*

ॐ वत्सराय नमः

He dwells in all in order to establish Dharma.

471. Vatsala: *The Affectionate*

ॐ वत्सलाय नमः

He has love and affection for His devotees.

472. Vatsi: *The Protector Of The People*

ॐ वत्सिने नमः

As the Father of the world, His children are dear to Him. Or, He is the protector of the people as of the calves in His incarnation as Krishna.

473. Ratnagarbha: *The Main*

ॐ रत्नगर्भाय नमः

In the form of the ocean, He is the repository of all gems.

474. Dhaneshwara: *The Lord Of Wealth*

ॐ धनेश्वराय नमः

As the Lord of wealth, He distributes wealth to sincere devotees like Kuchela.

475. Dharmagup: *The Protector Of Dharma*

ॐ धर्मगुपे नमः

He is born in every age for the establishment of Dharma.

476. Dharmakrut: *The Doer Of Dharma*

ॐ धर्मकृते नमः

Though transcending Dharma and Adharma, He acts only righteously to protect righteousness.

477. Dharmi: *The Supporter Of Dharma*

ॐ धर्मिणे नमः

He upholds Dharma and protects those who seek refuge in Him.

478. Sat: *Being*

ॐ सते नमः

He is the supreme Being, the Reality.

479. Asat: *The Conditioned*

ॐ असते नमः

He, in His conditioned aspect, is called *Asat*, meaning, He exists only in name as a mere play of words.

480. Ksharam: *Present In The Perishable*

ॐ क्षराय नमः

He is all beings (which perish ultimately) and is present in them.

481. Aksharam: *The Imperishable*

ॐ अक्षराय नमः

He is two-fold in the world—the perishable, made up of all creatures, and the imperishable.

482. Avijnata: *The Non-knower Of Objects*

ॐ अविज्ञात्रे नमः

The knower is the being who thinks that authorship and the rest pertain to Him; being free from it, is the Lord.

483. Sahasramshu: *The Thousand-rayed*

ॐ सहस्रांशवे नमः

The rays in the sun and other luminaries being His, He is the real Sun.

484. Vidhata: *The All-supporter*

ॐ विधात्रे नमः

He is the unique supporter of all beings, like Adishesha, Ananta, etc., which in turn support all else.

485. Krutalakshana: *The Eternal Consciousness*

ॐ कृतलक्षणाय नमः

The Vedas and other scriptures have originated from Him who is perfect, eternal Consciousness. Or, He has made in all beings the distinction of separation in their species as well as in others. Or, He bears the *shrivatsa* on His chest.

486. Gabhastinemi: *The Centre Of The Planetary Systems*

ॐ गभस्तिनेमये नमः

He dwells as the sun, in the centre of the circle of luminaries.

487. Sattvastha: *Abiding In Virtues*

ॐ सत्त्वस्थाय नमः

He resides in all beings. Or, He chiefly dwells in virtues which are radiant.

488. Simha: *The Lion*

ॐ सिंहाय नमः

He is valourous like the lion. Or, He may be Narasimha in His incarnation, the name being contracted to Simha.

489. Bhutamaheshwara: *The Great Lord Of Beings*

ॐ भूतमहेश्वराय नमः

He is the Supreme Lord of all beings. Or, As the Great Being, He presents Himself in the form of all beings.

490. Adideva: *The First Deity*

ॐ आदिदेवाय नमः

He is the 'first' through whom all beings come to exist.

491. Mahadeva: *The Great Deity*

ॐ महादेवाय नमः

He is the great Deity whose greatness consists in His supreme self-knowledge.

492. Devesha: *The Lord Of The Gods*

ॐ देवेशाय नमः

He is the Lord of all devas, and the most important among them.

493. Devabhrudguru: *The Ruler Of Indra*

ॐ देवभृद्गुरवे नमः

He is the Lord of Indra who is the Lord of the gods. Or, He is the support of the gods and promulgator of all lores.

494. Uttara: *The Saviour*

ॐ उत्तराय नमः

He is the Saviour from the ocean of samsara. Or, He is supreme over all.

495. Gopati: *The Cowherd*

ॐ गोपतये नमः

In His incarnation as Krishna, He tends the cows. Or, He is the Lord of the earth.

496. Gopta: *The Protector*

ॐ गोप्त्रे नमः

He is the Protector of all beings.

497. Gnanagamya: *Attained Only Through True Knowledge*

ॐ ज्ञानगम्याय नमः

He cannot be known through actions, or a combination of actions and knowledge; He can be known only through true knowledge.

498. Puratana: *The Ancient*

ॐ पुरातनाय नमः

Since He is unlimited by time, transcending it, He is the Ancient.

499. Sharirabhutabhrut: *The Nourisher Of The Body Elements*

ॐ शरीरभूतभृते नमः

Being the Vital Breath, He is the Master of the five elements comprising the body.

500. Bhokta: *The Protector Or Enjoyer*

ॐ भोक्त्रे नमः

He protects all beings. Or, He enjoys supreme Bliss.

501. Kapindra: *The Great Boar*

ॐ कपीन्द्राय नमः

He is manifested as Varaha in one incarnation. Or, In His Rama incarnation He was the Lord of monkeys.

502. Bhuridakshina: *The Bestower Of Large Gifts*

ॐ भूरिदक्षिणाय नमः

He encourages sacrificers to donate liberally to those who perform sacrifices, upholding the Dharma.

503. Somapa: *The Drinker Of Soma*

ॐ सोमपाय नमः

He quaffs the soma-juice in the form of the deity at sacrifices. Or, He drinks the soma as the sacrifice who conforms to Dharma.

504. Amrutapa: *The Drinker Of Ambrosia*

ॐ अमृतपाय नमः

He drinks the nectar of bliss which is of His Self. Or, He recovered the nectar from the demons and shared it with the gods.

505. Soma: *The Moon*

ॐ सोमाय नमः

Assuming the form of the moon, He invigorates the plants. Or, He is Shiva who is ever with Uma.

506. Purujit: *The Conqueror Of Many*

ॐ पुरुजिते नमः

He gains victory over many.

507. Purusattama: *The Omnipresent And Best*

ॐ पुरुसत्तमाय नमः

As He is of cosmic dimensions, He is Omnipresent, and He is the best.

508. Vinaya: *The Chastiser*

ॐ विनयाय नमः

He chastises the evil doers.

509. Jaya: *The Victorious*

ॐ जयाय नमः

He is victorious over all beings

510. Satyasandha: *Of Right Resolutions*

ॐ सत्यसंधाय नमः

Truth is His resolve.

511. Dasharha: *The Deserver Of Gifts*

ॐ दाशार्हाय नमः

He is the Divine to whom charitable offerings deserve to be made.
Or, He was born as Krishna in the Dasharha tribe of cowherds.

512. Satvatampati: *The Lord Of The Satvata*

ॐ सात्वतांपतये नमः

He confers good on and protects those who follow the Tantra
named *Satvata* which are scriptures sattvic in nature.

513. Jiva: *The Living Being*

ॐ जीवाय नमः

As He supports the senses in the form of the individual self, He is
the living Being.

514. Vinayitasakshi: *The Witness Of Modesty*

ॐ विनयितासाक्षिणे नमः

He witnesses the worshipful attitude of the devotees. Or, He, the
Omnipresent, does not witness anything outside Himself.

515. Mukunda: *The Bestower Of Salvation*

ॐ मुकुन्दाय नमः

He bestows salvation to the deserved.

516. Amitavikrama: *Of Immeasurable Prowess*

ॐ अमितविक्रमाय नमः

He is endowed with immeasurable prowess. Or, as Vamana, His three steps, transversing the whole universe were immeasurable.

517. Ambhonidhi: *The Abode Of Gods And Others*

ॐ अम्भोनिधये नमः

He is the abode in whom dwell the gods, men, manes and demons. Or, of all water bodies, He is the ocean.

518. Anantatma: *The Infinite Self*

ॐ अनन्तात्मने नमः

He cannot be limited or determined by time, space, and substance.

519. Mahodadhishaya: *The Recliner In The Great Ocean*

ॐ महोदधिशयाय नमः

He reclines in the primeval waters of cosmic Dissolution into which all entities in the universe have dissolved.

520. Antaka: *The End Of All*

ॐ अन्तकाय नमः

He brings about the end of all by the total withdrawal of the world.

521. Aja: *Love*

ॐ अजाय नमः

He is Love personified as Kama (Love) which was born of Him.

522. Maharha: *Deserving Worship*

ॐ महाहर्य नमः

He is the divine Being fit for worship.

523. Swabhavya: *The Unaffected*

ॐ स्वाभाव्याय नमः

Being eternally perfect, He is naturally without a beginning.

524. Jitamitra: *The Conqueror of Foes*

ॐ जितामित्राय नमः

He is the Conqueror of inner enemies like anger, pride, etc., and external enemies like Ravana, Kumbhakarna, etc.

525. Pramodana: *Ever Joyful*

ॐ प्रमोदनाय नमः

He is ever joyful as He is absorbed in immortal Bliss. Or, He confers bliss on those who meditate on Him, and this gives Him joy.

526. Ananda: *Bliss*

ॐ आनन्दाय नमः

He is pure Bliss.

527. Nandna: *The Source Of Happiness*

ॐ नन्दनाय नमः

He give pure delight and happiness..

528. Nanda: *Free Worldly Pleasures*

ॐ नन्दाय नमः

Being endowed with all perfections, He is free from wordly pleasures, and hence, rich in everything.

529. Satyadharma: *Of True Dharma*

ॐ सत्यधर्मणे नमः

His Knowledge and other attributes are true.

530. Trivikrama: *Of Three Steps*

ॐ त्रिविक्रमाय नमः

He triumphed over the worlds with His three steps. Or, He has walked over the three worlds.

531. Maharshi Kapilacharya: *Kapilacharya, The Great Sage*

ॐ महर्षये कपिलाचार्याय नमः

He was the great Rishi as He visioned the entire Vedas, whereas the others visioned only partly. Kapila was the teacher of pure truth, leading to enlightenment in the form of Samkhya. Among the perfected ones, He is the sage Kapila.

532. Krutajna: *The Universe And Its Knower*

ॐ कृतज्ञाय नमः

Since He created the universe, He is the knower or Atman.

533. Medinipati: *The Lord Of The Earth*

ॐ मेदिनीपतये नमः

Being the creator and withrawer, He is the Lord of the earth.

534. Tripada: *The Three-stepped*

ॐ त्रिपदाय नमः

He triumphed over the three worlds by His strides. Or, He is denoted by Om, Tat, Sat.

535. Tridashadhyaksha: *The Lord Of The Three Statets*

ॐ त्रिदशाध्यक्षाय नमः

He is the Lord of the three states of waking, dream and sleep, which come into being due to the three qualities.

536. Mahashringa: *The Great-horned*

ॐ महाश्रृंगाय नमः

In His incarnation as Matsaya, He sported a boat tied to His great horn, and played in the cosmic waters.

537. Krutantakrut: *The Withdrawer Of The Universe*

ॐ कृतान्तकृते नमः

He withdraws the universe during Dissolution. Or, He is the destroyer of death itself.

538. Mahavaraha: *The Great Boar*

ॐ महावराहाय नमः

He was the great Boar in His incarnations as Varaha.

539. Govinda: *Known By Scriptures*

ॐ गोविन्दाय नमः

He is so called as He is known through scriptural texts.

540. Sushena: *Having A Good Army*

ॐ सुषेणाय नमः

He has an armed guard in the form of divine hosts.

541. Kanakangadi: *Having Golden Armlets*

ॐ कनकाङ्गादिने नमः

He has armlets made of gold, or shining golden.

542. Guhya: *The Mysterious*

ॐ गुह्याय नमः

He is to be known by the esoteric knowledge conveyed by the *Upanishads*. Or, He is hidden in the *guha* or the ether of the heart.

543. Gabhira: *The Unfathomable*

ॐ गभीराय नमः

He is profound majesty in His wisdom, strength, supremacy, etc.

544. Gahana: *The Impenetrable*

ॐ गहनाय नमः

He is impenetrables as He is free from, or witness to, the three states of waking, dream, and sleep, and their absence.

545. Gupta: *The Concealed*

ॐ गुप्ताय नमः

Being hidden in all beings, He is not manifested.

546. Chakragadadhara: *The Bearer Of Chakra And Gada*

ॐ चक्रगदाधराय नमः

He bears the chakra or discus, symbolising the mind-aspect, and the gada or mace, symbolising the intellect-aspect.

547. Vedha: *The Originator*

ॐ वेधसे नमः

He is the cause and originator of all.

548. Svanga: *Self-instrument*

ॐ सवाङ्गाय नमः

He is the auxiliary cause of the creation, and hence, self-instrumental.

549. Ajita: *The Unconquered*

ॐ अजिताय नमः

He has not been conquered by anyone in His various incarnations.

550. Krishna: *The Dark (Vyasa)*

ॐ कृष्णाय नमः

Vyasa, the author of the *Mahabharata* was none other than the lotus-eyed Lord Himself.

551. Drudha: *The Firm*

ॐ दृढाय नमः

He is firm in His nature and capacity which knows no decay.

552. Sankarshanochyuta: *The Withdrawing And The Unswering*

ॐ संकर्षणायाच्युताय नमः

He draws in during Dissolution all the world, and is unswerving in His own nature.

553. Varuna: *The Withholder*

ॐ वरूणाय नमः

The setting sun, called Varuna, withdraws his rays into himself, and the Lord is this Varuna.

554. Vaaruna: *The Son Of Varuna*

ॐ वारुणाय नमः

In His partial incarnation, He is either Vasishtha or Agastya (sons of Varuna).

555. Vriksha: *The Tree*

ॐ वृक्षाय नमः

He alone stands in the spiritual dimension, unmoving like a tree.

556. Pushkaraksha: *Pervader Of The Lotus Of The Heart*

ॐ पुष्कराक्षाय नमः

He shines as the light of consciousness when meditated upon in the lotus of the heart. Or, He pervades the lotus of the heart.

557. Mahamana: *Of Great Mind*

ॐ महामनसे नमः

He with His mind alone creates and dissolves the universe.

558. Bhagavan: *The Blessed*

ॐ भगवते नमः

He alone possesses the six attributes of lordliness, Dharma, fame, wealth, dispassion, and salvation.

559. Bhagagna: *The Remover Of Wealth, etc.*

ॐ भगघ्ने नमः

He withdraws all the attributes into Himself during the Dissolution.

560. Anandi: *The Delighter*

ॐ अनन्दिने नमः

Being Himself Bliss, He delights all. Or, He delights all as He is rich in everything.

561. Vanamali: *Wearing The Vanamala*

ॐ वनमालिने नमः

He wears the vanamala or floral wreath called Vaijayanti, symbolising the five elements.

562. Halayudha: *Armed With A Plough*

ॐ हलायुधाय नमः

In His incarnation as Balarama, He had a plough as His weapon.

563. Aditya: *Born Of Aditi*

ॐ अदित्याय नमः

In this incarnation as Vamana, He was born of Aditi.

564. Jyotiraditya: *The Deity In The Sun*

ॐ ज्योतिरादित्याय नमः

He is the deity residing in the disc of the sun. Or, He is the brilliant luminary, the sun.

565. Sahishnu: *The Endurer*

ॐ सहिष्णवे नमः

He endures all contraries like heat and cold, etc.

566. Gatisattama: *The Refuge And The Best*

ॐ गतिसत्तमाय नमः

He is the ultimate resort and support of all, and the best among all beings.

567. Sudhanva: *With A Good Bow*

ॐ सुधन्वाय नमः

He is armed with a good bow named Sharnga, symbolising the senses, eyes and the rest.

568. Khandaparashu: *With A Punishing Axe*

ॐ खण्डपरशवे नमः

During His incarnation as Parashurama, the son of Gamadagni, He punished the foes with His axe.

569. Daruna: *Hard*

ॐ दारुणाय नमः

He is hard and merciless to the evil-doers.

570. Dravinaprada: *The Giver Of Wealth*

ॐ द्रविणप्रदाय नमः

He bestows the desired wealth on devotees.

571. Divasprush: *The Sky-reaching*

ॐ दिवस्पृशे नमः

One reaches heaven by supreme knowledge, and Lord Vishnu is the goal for the seekers of this knowledge.

572. Sarvadrigvyasa: *Omniscient Vyasa*

ॐ सर्वदृग्व्यासाय नमः

He is One whose comprehension includes everything in its ambit. Or, He is the power of comprehension in all. As Vyasa, He divided the Vedas into four; He divided the Rigveda, the Yajurveda, the Samaveda, and the Atharvaveda into twenty-one, hundred and one, thousand, and nine branches, respectively; hence, Vyasa means Creator.

573. Vachaspatirayonija: *The Unborn Lord Of Vidyas*

ॐ वाचस्पतयेऽयोनिजाय नमः

He is the Master of all learning, and not born of any mother.

574. Trisama: *Having The Three Samas*

ॐ त्रिसाम्ने नमः

He is praised by the singers of the three *Samas*, which are the hymns of the Samaveda.

575. Samaga: *The Singer Of Saman*

ॐ सामगाय नमः

He is the great Singer of the Samaveda hymns.

576. Sama: *The Samaveda*

ॐ साम्ने नमः

Of the Vedas, He is the Samaveda.

577. Nirvanam: *Final Liberation*

ॐ निर्वाणाय नमः

He is of the nature of supreme Bliss, free of all sorrows.

578. Bheshajam: *The Medicine*

ॐ भेषजाय नमः

He is the antidote for the diseases of worldly ills (samsara).

579. Bhishak: *The Physician*

ॐ भिषजे नमः

Through the *Bhagavad Gita*, He taught the supreme knowledge which is the medicine to cure all diseases of samsara.

580. Sannyasakrut: *The Institutor Of The Sannyasa Stage*

ॐ संन्यासकृते नमः

He is responsible for instituting the fourth stage, ashrama, for the attainment of salvation.

581. Shama: *The Quiescence*

ॐ शमाय नमः

He ordained the principle of 'calmness' to the ascetics as the necessary means towards wisdom.

582. Shanta: *The Quiescence*

ॐ शान्ताय नमः

He is always tranquil, being free from involvement in material pleasures.

583. Nishtha: *The Stable Abode*

ॐ निष्ठायै नमः

During the time of Dissolution, all beings who have shed their desires, seek refuge in Him.

584. Shanti: *The Peace*

ॐ शान्त्यै नमः

He is beyond ignorance, and every form of nescience.

585. Parayanam: *The Supreme Goal*

ॐ परायणाय नमः

He is the highest State from which there is no return.

586. Shubhanga: *The Handsome*

ॐ शुभाङ्गाय नमः

He is endowed with a handsome form.

587. Shantida: *The Bestower Of Peace*

ॐ शान्तिदाय नमः

He bestows peace which is the state of freedom from attachment, etc.

588. Srashta: *The Creator*

ॐ स्रष्टे नमः

He is the Creator of everything in the very beginning.

589. Kumuda: *The Delighter In The Earth*

ॐ कुमुदाय नमः

During His incarnations, He delights in the earth.

590. Kuvaleshaya: *The Recliner Upon The Waters*

ॐ कुवलेशयाय नमः

He reclines on the divine serpent, Shesha, upon the waters.

591. Gohita: *The Friend Of The Cows*

ॐ गोहिताय नमः

He, as Krishna, protected the cows from the torrential rain by lifting the Govardhana mount. Or, He incarnated to lighten the earth by slaying the demons.

592. Gopati: *The Lord Of The Earth*

ॐ गोपतये नमः

He is the Lord of the earth, as also of the senses.

593. Gopta: *The Protector*

ॐ गोप्त्रे नमः

He is the Protector of the universe. Or, He conceals Himself by His Maya.

594. Vrishabhaksha: *Dharma-eyed*

ॐ वृषभाक्षाय नमः

His eyes shower the fulfilment of all wishes.

595. Vrishapriya: *Delighting In Dharma*

ॐ वृषप्रियाय नमः

To Him, Dharma is dear. Or, He is Dharma Himself which is beloved of all.

596. Anivarti: *Never Retreating*

ॐ अनिवर्तिने नमः

He never retreats in the wars with the demons. Or, Being devoted to Dharma, He never turns back from it.

597. Nivrittatma: *Of Restrained Self*

ॐ निवृत्तात्मने नमः

He is naturally turned away from material pleasures.

598. Sankshepta: *Compressor*

ॐ संक्षेप्त्रे नमः

During the Dissolution, He contracts the universe into its subtle form.

599. Kshemakrut: *The Preserver Of Welfare*

ॐ क्षेमकृते नमः

He protects the welfare of those that abandon themselves to Him.

600. Shiva: *The Purifier*

ॐ शिवाय नमः

He purifies those that even utter or remember His name.

601. Shrivatsavaksha: *With The Shrivatsa On His Breast*

ॐ श्रीवत्सवक्षसे नमः

He has the mark *Shrivatsa,* a curl of hair, on His breast.

602. Shrivasa: *The Abode Of Shri*

ॐ श्रीवासाय नमः

On His chest dwells Lakshmi (Shri) forever.

603. Shripati: *The Lord Of Shri*

ॐ श्रीपतये नमः

Shri or Lakshmi chose Him as her husband during the churning of the ocean for nectar. Or, He is the Lord of Shri, the Shakti, or Supreme Power.

604. Shrimatamvara: *The Chief Of Those Possessing The Vedas*

ॐ श्रीमतांवराय नमः

He is the chief of Brahma and others who possess the Vedas.

605. Shrida: *The Bestower Of Wealth*

ॐ श्रीदाय नमः

He bestows wealth on His devotees.

606. Shrisha: *The Lord Of Wealth*

ॐ श्रीशाय नमः

He is the Lord of wealth, as well as of Shri (Lakshmi).

607. Shrinivasa: *Ever Abiding In The Well-endowed*

ॐ श्रीनिवासाय नमः

He always dwells in the virtuous and humble.

608. Shrinidhi: *The Treasure-house Of Shri*

ॐ श्रीनिधये नमः

He is the gold mine in which all energies abide.

609. Shrivibhavana: *The Distributor Of Wealth*

ॐ श्रीविभावनाय नमः

He distributes the just rewards to all according to their acts.

78

610. Shridhara: *Bearing Shri On His Chest*

ॐ श्रीधराय नमः

He bears on His chest the mother of all, Lakshmi.

611. Shrikara: *The Bestower Of Virtues*

ॐ श्रीकराय नमः

He confers virtues on those who worship, praise, and remember Him.

612. Shreya: *Salvation*

ॐ श्रेयसे नमः

He is Salvation which gives one eternal Bliss.

613. Shriman: *The Possessor Of Shri*

ॐ श्रीमते नमः

He possesses all virtues, power, splendour, and supreme wisdom.

614. Lokatrayashraya: *The Refuge Of The Three Worlds*

ॐ लोकत्रयाश्रयाय नमः

He is the refuge of the three worlds comprising the earth, the atmospheric region and the heavens.

615. Swaksha: *Beautiful-eyed*

ॐ स्वक्षाय नमः

His eyes are beautiful like lotus-petals.

616. Swanga: *Beautiful-limbed*

ॐ स्वङ्गाय नमः

His limbs are beautiful especially as Rama and Krishna.

617. Shatananda: *Of Infinite Bliss*

ॐ शतानन्दाय नमः

He is of infinite Bliss, of which others enjoy only a small part.

618. Nandi: *The Embodiment Of Supreme Bliss*

ॐ नन्दये नमः

He is of the nature of supreme Bliss.

619. Jyotirganeshwara: *The Lord Of The Luminaries*

ॐ ज्योतिर्गणेऽवराय नमः

Everything shines by His effulgence, and when He shines, others shine after Him.

620. Vijitatma: *The Mind-subduer*

ॐ विजितात्मने नमः

He conquers the mind and subdues it.

621. Avidheyatma: *Of Unfathomed Nature*

ॐ अविधेयात्मने नमः

No one, unless liberated, knows His true nature.

622. Satkirti: *Of True Fame*

ॐ सत्कीर्तये नमः

His fame is true and supreme.

623. Chinnasamshaya: *Free From Doubts*

ॐ छिन्नसंशयाय नमः

He has no doubts whatsoever, He being able to perceive everything clearly.

624. Udirna: *Transcendent*

ॐ उदीर्णाय नमः

He is beyond everything as He is superior to all.

625. Sarvatashchakshu: *Having Eyes Everywhere*

ॐ सर्वतश्चक्षुषे नमः

Being pure Consciousness, He can see everything in all directions.

626. Anisha: *Having No Lord Over Him*

ॐ अनीशाय नमः

There is none who is His master.

627. Shashvatasthira: *Eternal And Stable*

ॐ शाऽवतस्थिराय नमः

He is eternal and unchanging.

80

628. Bhushaya: *Resting On The Ground*

ॐ भूशयाय नमः

In His Rama avatara, He rested on the shores of the ocean on His journey to Lanka.

629. Bhushana: *Adorning The World*

ॐ भूषणाय नमः

He adorned the world by His various incarnations.

630. Bhuti: *Glorious*

ॐ भूतये नमः

He is the source of all glories. Or, He is the essence of everything.

631. Vishoka: *The Griefless*

ॐ विशोकाय नमः

Being absolute Bliss, He is free of grief.

632. Shokanashana: *The Destroyer Of Grief*

ॐ शोकनाशनाय नमः

By their very remembrance of Him, the devotees are free of grief.

633. Archishman: *The Brilliant*

ॐ अर्चिष्मते नमः

He is the brilliant Lord by whose radiance other luminaries shine.

634. Archita: *The Worshipped*

ॐ अर्चिताय नमः

All, including Brahma, worship Him.

635. Kumbha: *The Container*

ॐ कुम्भाय नमः

He contains in Himself everything, as in a pot.

636. Vishuddhatma: *The Pure Atman*

ॐ विशुद्धात्मने नमः

The Lord, free from all impurities, is above *Sattva*, *Rajas*, and *Tamas*.

637. Vishodhana: *The Purifier*

ॐ विशोधनाय नमः

He purifies all sins if the devotees merely remember Him.

638. Aniruddha: *The Unobstructed*

ॐ अनिरुद्धाय नमः

He cannot be obstructed by enemies, being the fourth of the four manifestations — Vasudeva, Samkarshana, Pradyumna and Aniruddha.

639. Apratiratha: *The Unrivalled*

ॐ अप्रतिरथाय नमः

He has no equal or anyone above Him.

640. Pradyumna: *With Wealth Of A Sacred Order*

ॐ प्रद्युम्नाय नमः

His Wealth is superior and sacred. Or, He is one of the four *Vyuhas*.

641. Amitavikrama: *Of Unequalled Powers*

ॐ अमितविक्रमाय नमः

His prowess is unlimited. Or, His prowess cannot be obstructed by anyone.

642. Kalaneminiha: *The Slayer Of Kalanemi*

ॐ कालनेमिघ्ने नमः

He slew the demon Kalanemi, the grandson of Hiranyakashipu.

643. Vira: *The Valiant*

ॐ वीराय नमः

He is courageous and bold.

644. Shauri: *Born Of The Shura Clan*

ॐ शौरये नमः

As Krishna, He was born in the Shura clan of the Yadavas.

645. Shurajaneshwara: *The Lord Of The Valiant*

ॐ शूरजनेᳶवराय नमः

By His overwhelming prowess, He controls even powers like Indra and others.

646. Trilokatma: *The Self Of The Three Worlds*

ॐ त्रिलोकात्मे नमः

As the Self, He controls the three worlds. Or, The three worlds do not exist without Him.

647. Trilokesha: *Three Worlds*

ॐ त्रिलोकेशाय नमः

Under His guidance, everything in the three worlds functions.

648. Keshava: *Whose Hair Is Effulgence*

ॐ केशवाय नमः

The rays in the luminaries are owned by Him. Or, He rules over energies called Brahma, Rudra and Vishnu. His hair, dark and white (called Shakti) are on the earth. Or, 'Ka' meaning Brahma, and 'Isha' meaning Lord of all embodied things, are born of Him.

649. Keshiha: *The Slayer Of Keshin*

ॐ केशिघ्ने नमः

As Krishna, He slew the demon, Keshin.

650. Hari: *The Withholder*

ॐ हरये नमः

He wards off the evils of samsara from His devotees.

651. Kamadeva: *The Beloved Lord*

ॐ कामदेवाय नमः

He is the desired Lord of all.

652. Kamapala: *The Fulfiller Of Desires*

ॐ कामपालाय नमः

He fulfils the desires of those who devotedly seek Him.

653. Kami: *Of Fulfilled Desires*

ॐ कामिने नमः

His desires are always concerning His devotees.

654. Kanta: *Handsome*

ॐ कान्ताय नमः

In His incarnations He assumes handsome forms. Or, He is the cause of the end of Brahma at the close of the second half of his age.

655. Kritagama: *The Author Of The Agamas*

ॐ कृतागमाय नमः

He is responsible for scriptures like the Agamas, Vedas, Shastras, etc.

656. Anirdeshyavapu: *Of Indescribable Form*

ॐ अनिर्देश्यवपुषे नमः

His form cannot be defined, as He is above all attributes.

657. Vishnu: *Of Pervasive Effulgence*

ॐ विष्णवे नमः

His radiance pervades the firmament and transcends it.

658. Vira: *The Swift-mover*

ॐ वीराय नमः

He has the power to move swiftly into the heart of devotees or against demons.

659. Ananta: *Infinite*

ॐ अनन्ताय नमः

He is unlimited by space, time or substance, being all-pervading.

660. Dhananjaya: *The Conqueror Of Wealth*

ॐ धनंजयाय नमः

Arjuna, a glorious manifestation of the Lord, won immense wealth from his campaigns.

661. Brahmanya: *The Friend Of Brahman*

ॐ ब्रह्मण्याय नमः

The Lord promotes penance, Vedas, and beings well-versed in scriptures.

662. Brahmakrut: *The Author Of Brahman*

ॐ ब्रह्मकृते नमः

He is responsible for all austerities, etc.

663. Brahma: *The Creator*

ॐ ब्रह्मणे नमः

He, as Brahma, creates all.

664. Brahma: *Reality*

ॐ ब्रह्मणे नमः

As He is great and all-pervading, He is characterised by be-ness, knowledge, infinite.

665. Brahmavivardhana: *The Increaser Of Brahman*

ॐ ब्रह्मविवर्धनाय नमः

He promotes austerities, etc.

666. Brahmavit: *The Knower Of Brahman*

ॐ ब्रह्मविदे नमः

He knows the Vedas and their meaning.

667. Brahmana: *The Interpreter Of Brahman*

ॐ ब्राह्मणाय नमः

He instructs the world through the Brahman or Vedas.

668. Brahmi: *The Prime Possessor Of Brahman*

ॐ ब्रह्मिणे नमः

He possesses, besides the Vedas, other specific aspects also.

669. Brahmajna: *The Knower Of Brahman*

ॐ ब्रह्मज्ञाय नमः

He knows the Vedas which are in Himself.

85

670. Brahmanapriya: *The Beloved Of Brahmanas*

ॐ ब्राह्मणप्रियाय नमः

He is the beloved friend of devoted holy men.

671. Mahakrama: *Of Wide Steps*

ॐ महाक्रमाय नमः

He takes good steps to spread devotion to Him.

672. Mahakarma: *Of Grand Deeds*

ॐ महाकर्मणे नमः

He performs great deeds like creation, etc.

673. Mahateja: *Of Great Radiance*

ॐ महातेजसे नमः

He, by whom other luminaries shine, is of great radiance.

674. Mahoraga: *The Great Serpent*

ॐ महोरगाय नमः

Among serpents, He is Vasuki, the great serpent.

675. Mahakratu: *The Great Sacrifice*

ॐ महाक्रतवे नमः

Just as the *Ashwamedha* is the chief of sacrifices, He is Himself such a great sacrifice.

676. Mahayajva: *The Great Sacrificer*

ॐ महायज्वाने नमः

He performs great sacrifices for the well-being of the universe.

677. Mahayajna: *The Great Sacrifice*

ॐ महायज्ञाय नमः

Among the sacrifices, He is the Japa-yajna in which there is silent repetition of chants.

678. Mahahavi: *The Great Offering*

ॐ महाहविषे नमः

The whole universe is rendered as an offering to Brahman, it being the Self.

679. Stavya: *The Object Of Praise*

ॐ स्तव्याय नमः

He is praised by all but He praises none.

680. Stavapriya: *Delighting In Praise*

ॐ स्तवप्रियाय नमः

He is pleased with hymns and praises.

681. Stotram: *The Hymn*

ॐ स्तोत्राय नमः

The hymn which describes His virtues and attributes is Lord Vishnu Himself.

682. Stuti: *The Act Of Praise*

ॐ स्तुतये नमः

This act of praise too is Lord Vishnu Himself.

683. Stota: *The Eulogiser*

ॐ स्तोत्रे नमः

Being the Self of all, He sings a hymn of praise.

684. Ranapriya: *Delighting In Battles*

ॐ रणप्रियाय नमः

Armed with the various weapons, He delights in battles.

685. Purna: *The Self-fulfilled*

ॐ पूर्णाय नमः

Being the source of all powers and excellence, He is the Plenum.

686. Purayita: *The Fulfiller*

ॐ पूरयित्रे नमः

He, being Self-fulfilled, gives fulfilment to others.

687. Punya: *The Holy*

ॐ पुण्याय नमः

He removes sins by the very remembrance of Him.

688. Punyakirti: *Of Holy Fame*

ॐ पुण्यकीर्तये नमः

His fame bestows holiness on beings.

689. Anamaya: *The Ever-healthy*

ॐ अनामयाय नमः

He is free from afflictions born of causes, both internal and external.

690. Manojava: *Fleet As The Mind*

ॐ मनोजवाय नमः

Being all-pervading, He is as fast as the mind.

691. Tirthakara: *The Teacher Of The Vidyas*

ॐ तीर्थकराय नमः

He, being the source of the fourteen *vidyas* mentioned in the Vedas, imparted all the Vedas to Brahma, and all the *vidyas* outside the pale of the Vedas to the demons to deceive them.

692. Vasureta: *One Whose Essence Is Gold.*

ॐ वसुरेतसे नमः

He created the waters, and cast His power into them. It became the golden Egg from which Brahma was born.

693. Vasuprada: *The Giver Of Wealth*

ॐ वसुप्रदाय नमः

He gladly bestows wealth in abundance, and Kubera became the lord of wealth only through His grace.

694. Vasuprada: *The Bestower Of Salvation*

ॐ वसुप्रदाय नमः

He bestows the greatest wealth, salvation, on the deserving. Or, He deprives the demons of their wealth.

695. Vasudeva: *The Son Of Vasudeva*

ॐ वासुदेवाय नमः

In His incarnation as Krishna, He was Vasudeva's son.

696. Vasu: *The Refuge Of All*

ॐ वसवे नमः

All beings dwell in Him, as He in them.

697. Vasumana: *Of Omnipresent Mind*

ॐ वसुमनसे नमः

His mind dwells equally, without distinction, in all things.

698. Havi: *The Oblation*

ॐ हविषे नमः

He is the offering and He is the oblation.

699. Sadgati: *The Refuge Of The Good*

ॐ सद्गतये नमः

He is the refuge sought by the good. Or, He is of superior intellect.

700. Satkruti: *Of Good Acts*

ॐ सत्कृतये नमः

All His good acts are for the benefit of the universe.

701. Satta: *Being*

ॐ सत्तायै नमः

He is the only One, without a second.

702. Sadbhuti: *Unsublated Being*

ॐ सदभूतये नमः

He, being pure Existence and Consciousness, is unsublated Being.

703. Satparayana: *The Supreme Goal Of The Good*

ॐ सत्परायणाय नमः

He is the highest goal attainable by those who have realised the Truth.

704. Shurasena: *Owning Valiant Armies*

ॐ शूरसेनाय नमः

He, in His various incarnations, had valiant heroes like Hanuman.

705. Yadushreshtha: *The Chief Of The Yadus*

ॐ यदुश्रेष्ठाय नमः

As Krishna, He was the Chief of the Yadu clan.

706. Sannivasa: *The Abode Of The Wise*

ॐ सन्निवासाय नमः

He is the resort sought by the wise.

707. Suyamuna: *Attended By Good Yamunas*

ॐ सुयामुनाय नमः

He is surrounded and attended by such illustrious people like Vasudeva, Devaki, Yashoda, Balarama, Subhadra, etc., who are associated with the Yamuna river. Or, His cowherd attendants are Brahma and others in human form.

708. Bhutavasa: *The Dwelling Place Of Beings*

ॐ भूतावासाय नमः

All beings dwell in Him.

709. Vasudeva: *Divinity Enveloping The Universe With Maya*

ॐ वासुदेवाय नमः

Like the sun's rays cover the whole earth, so His Maya covers the whole universe.

710. Sarvasunilaya: *The Abode Of Like-energies*

ॐ सर्वासुनिलयाय नमः

He is the Abode in whom all the vital energies dissolve.

711. Anala: *The Unlimited*

ॐ अनलाय नमः

He has unlimited energies and power.

712. Darpaha: *The Represser Of Pride*

ॐ दर्पघ्ने नमः

He curbs the pride of those who stray from the righteous path.

713. Darpada: *The Giver Of Pride*

ॐ दर्पदाय नमः

He gives pride and dignity to those who follow the righteous path.
Or, He represses the pride of the erring.

714. Drupta: *The Exalted*

ॐ दृप्ताय नमः

He is ever satisfied enjoying His own inherent Bliss.

715. Durdhara: *The Object Of Hard Contemplation*

ॐ दुर्धराय नमः

It is very difficult to focus one's mind on Him, as He is without
any adjuncts or fields of manifestation.

716. Aparajita: *The Unconquered*

ॐ अपराजिताय नमः

He remains unconquered by enemies, desires, etc.

717. Vishwamurti: *The Universal Form*

ॐ विश्वमूर्तये नमः

Being the universal Self, He has the universal form.

718. Mahamurti: *The Great Form*

ॐ महामूर्तये नमः

He assumes a great form while reclining on the Adishesha couch.

719. Diptamurti: *Of Blazing Form*

ॐ दीप्तमूर्तये नमः

He has a luminous form of supreme wisdom. Or, His radiant form
is assumed at His own will.

720. Amurtiman: *The Formless*

ॐ अमूर्तिमते नमः

He is without a body brought on by karma.

721. Anekamurti: *Of Many Forms*

ॐ अनेकमूर्तये नमः

He assumes various forms in His many incarnations in order to help the world.

722. Avyakta: *Unmanifest*

ॐ अव्यक्ताय नमः

Though He manifests in various forms, He cannot be clearly described.

723. Shatamurti: *Of Myriad Forms*

ॐ शतमूर्तये नमः

He has myriad forms, created of His own free will.

724. Shatanana: *Myriad-faced*

ॐ शताननाय नमः

The whole universe is His form with myriad faces.

725. Eka: *The One*

ॐ एकस्मै नमः

There is only One, without a second.

726. Naika: *The Many*

ॐ नैकस्मै नमः

He sports with many forms by His maya.

727. Sava: *The Soma Sacrifice*

ॐ सवाय नमः

He is the Soma sacrifice where the juice of the soma plant is offered.

728. Ka: *Happiness*

ॐ काय नमः

He is happiness and brightness.

729. Kim: *What? (Brahman) What?*

ॐ कस्मै नमः

He is fit to be contemplated upon, as He is the summation of all values.

730. Yat: *Which (Brahman)*

ॐ यस्मै नमः

From whom or which all these beings come.

731. Tat: *That (Brahman)*

ॐ तस्मै नमः

That which (or Brahman who) pervades everywhere.

732. Padamanuttamam: *The Unequalled Status*

ॐ पदायानुत्तमाय नमः

He is the highest unequalled status which is sought by all.

733. Lokabandhu: *The Support Of The Universe*

ॐ लोकबन्धवे नमः

In Him all the worlds are linked as He is their support. Or, He is the support of all as He is the father of the worlds, no friend being equal to a father. Or, Through *shruti* and *smriti* He instructs the world in right and wrong.

734. Lokanatha: *The Lord Of The Universe*

ॐ लोकनाथाय नमः

All the worlds pray to Him. Or, He shines in, or blesses, or rules the world.

735. Madhava: *Madhu's Offspring*

ॐ माधवाय नमः

As Krishna, He was born in the family of Madhu, a Yadava.

736. Bhaktavatsala: *Affectionate To His Devotees*

ॐ भक्तवत्सलाय नमः

He has a lot of love for His devotees.

737. Suvarnavarna: *Golden-hued*

ॐ सुवर्णवर्णाय नमः

He appears golden-hued to the beholder.

738. Hemanga: *With Limbs Like Gold*

ॐ हेमाङ्गाय नमः

His form, golden-hued, has limbs like gold.

739. Varanga: *With Beautiful limbs*

ॐ वराङ्गाय नमः

His limbs are beautiful and golden.

740. Chandangadi: *With Attractive Armlets*

ॐ चन्दनाङ्गदिने नमः

He is adorned with attractive armlets that generate joy.

741. Viraha: *The Slayer Of Valiant Foes*

ॐ वीरघ्ने नमः

He destroys heroic foes like Hiranyakashipu to establish Dharma.

742. Vishama: *Unequalled*

ॐ विषमाय नमः

He is unequalled, as He transcends all.

743. Shunya: *Void (of Attributes)*

ॐ शून्याय नमः

He is like a void, as He is attributeless.

744. Ghrutashi: *He Who Makes No Request*

ॐ घृताशिषे नमः

His blessings are unfailing, though He makes no request.

745. Achala: *The Immutable*

ॐ अचलाय नमः

He undergoes no change in His wisdom, nature, etc.

746. Chala: *The Mutable*

ॐ चलाय नमः

He moves in His aspect as Vayu (air).

747. Amani: *The Egoless*

ॐ अमानिने नमः

Devoid of any ego, He has no sense of identification with anything that is not Atman.

748. Manada: *One Who Generates Egoistic Consciousness*

ॐ मानदाय नमः

By His power of maya, He induces the sense of self in non-self. Or, He bestows rewards upon His devotees. Or, He prevents rewards to evil-doers. Or, He destroys wrong notions of Atman in His devotees.

749. Manya: *Adored By All*

ॐ मान्याय नमः

He, being the Lord of all, is adored by them.

750. Lokaswami: *The Lord Of the Universe*

ॐ लोकस्वामिने नमः

He is the Lord of the fourteen worlds (seven above and seven below).

751. Trilokadhruk: *The Supporter Of The Three Worlds*

ॐ त्रिलोकाधृषे नमः

He supports all the three worlds.

752. Sumedha: *Of Bright Intelligence*

ॐ सुमेधसे नमः

He has bright and beneficent intelligence.

753. Medhaja: *Born In The Sacrifice*

ॐ मेधजाय नमः

He arose from the sacrifice.

754. Dhanya: *The Fortunate*

ॐ धन्याय नमः

He is fortunate because His objects are fulfilled.

755. Satyamedha: *Of Unfailing Intelligence*

ॐ सत्यमेधसे नमः

His intelligence, never failing, is fruitful.

756. Dharadhara: *The Support Of The Earth*

ॐ धराधराय नमः

He supports the worlds in the form of parts like Adishesha, etc.

757. Tejovrusha: *He Who Showers Rain*

ॐ तेजोवृषाय नमः

In the form of the sun, He showers rain.

758. Dyutidhara: *The Bearer Of Radiance*

ॐ द्युतिधराय नमः

In His incarnations, He had radiance in His limbs.

759. Sarvashastrabhrutamvara: *The Best Of Weapon-wielders*

ॐ सर्वशस्त्रभृतांवराय नमः

He is the best among all those who wield weapons.

760. Pragraha: *The Receiver*

ॐ प्रग्रहाय नमः

He accepts offerings with great delight. Or, He is like the reins which control horse-like senses running wild.

761. Nigraha: *The Controller*

ॐ निग्रहाय नमः

He controls and destroys everything.

762. Vyagra: *Devoid Of End*

ॐ व्यग्राय नमः

He is infinite and has no end. Or, He is always attentive on fulfilling the desires of His devotees.

763. Naikashringa: *The Many-horned*

ॐ नैकशृङ्गाय नमः

He, the Sacrificer, has four horns in the form of the Vedas.

764. Gadagraja: *Born Of Mantra*

ॐ गदग्रजाय नमः

He is revealed first by mantra in the Putrakameshthi sacrifice as Rama. Or, He was the elder brother of Gada (the younger brother of Krishna).

765. Chaturmurti: *Of Four Forms*

ॐ चतुर्मूर्तये नमः

He has four aspects — Viryj, Sutratman, Anyakrita and Turiya. Or, He has white, red, yellow and dark-blue bodies.

766. Chaturbahu: *The Four-Armed*

ॐ चतुर्बाहवे नमः

He has four arms, as Vasudeva is always described.

767. Chaturvyuha: *Having Four Manifestations*

ॐ चतुर्व्यूहाय नमः

The four manifestations are: Purusha in the body, in the Chandas, in the Vedas, and the great Purusha.

768. Chaturgati: *The Goal Of The Four*

ॐ चतुर्गतये नमः

He is sought as the goal by the four stages of life and the four castes ordained by the scriptures.

769. Chaturatma: *The Clear-minded*

ॐ चतुरात्मने नमः

Since He is free from desire, etc., He is clear-minded. Or, He has the fourfold mind-intellect-ego-mindstuff.

770. Chaturbhava: *The Source Of The Four*

ॐ चतुर्भावाय नमः

He is the source of pleasure, wealth, righteousness, and liberation.

771. Chaturvedavit: *The Knower Of The Four Vedas*

ॐ चतुर्वेदविदे नमः

He knows the Vedas as He is their author.

772. Ekapat: *The One-footed*

ॐ एकपदे नमः

He stands supporting the whole world by a part of Himself.

773. Samavarta: *The Skilful Turner*

ॐ समावर्ताय नमः

He deftly turns the wheel of worldly life.

774. Anivrittatma: *He Who Never Turns Away*

ॐ अनिवृत्तात्मने नमः

Being all-pervading, He never turns away. Or, He is turned away from objects of senses.

775. Durjaya: *The Invincible*

ॐ दुर्जयाय नमः

He can never be conquered.

776. Duratikrama: *Never Transgressed*

ॐ दुरतिक्रमाय नम

Being the source of fear, none dare disobey Him.

777. Durlabha: *Hard To Realise*

ॐ दुर्लभाय नमः

Only through rare devotion can He be realised.

778. Durgama: *Known With Difficulty*

ॐ दुर्गमाय नमः

He is difficult to know and attain.

779. Durga: *Not Easily Realised*

ॐ दुर्गाय नमः

Obstacles and difficulties make it hard to realise Him.

780. Duravasa: *Not Easily Retained*

ॐ दुरावासाय नमः

Devotees find it very difficult to bring Him to reside in their hearts in Samadhi.

781. Durariha: *The Slayer Of Wicked Enemies*

ॐ दुरारिघ्ने नमः

He slays wicked enemies like the demons.

782. Shubhanga: *Of Beautiful Limbs*

ॐ शुभाङ्गाय नमः

He is to be meditated upon as having beautiful limbs.

783. Lokasaranga: *He Who Grasps The Essence Of The World*

ॐ लोकसारङ्गाय नमः

He takes the essence of the universe, like a bee takes honey from flowers. Or, He is to be known through Pranava (the sound symbol 'Om').

784. Sutantu: *Beautifully Expanded*

ॐ सुतन्तवे नमः

He, like the universe, is beautifully expanded.

785. Tantuvardhana: *The Enhancer Of The Expanded Universe*

ॐ तन्तुवर्धनाय नमः

He can expand the world. Or, He can withdraw the world.

786. Indrakarma: *Resembling Indra In His Actions*

ॐ इन्द्रकर्मणे नमः

His actions, like Indra's, are great and glorious.

787. Mahakarma: *Of Great Deeds*

ॐ महाकर्मणे नमः

His great effects are the ether and other elements.

788. Krutakarma: *Of Fulfilled Activities*

ॐ कृताकर्मणे नमः

He has nothing more to achieve as all His activities are fulfilled. Or, He has performed virtuous deeds in His incarnations.

789. Krutagama: *The Author Of The Vedas*

ॐ कृतागमाय नमः

The Veda is what has been given by Him.

790. Udbhava: *Of Superior Birth*

ॐ उद्भवाय नमः

Being born of His own free will, whenever He likes, He is of superior birth. Or, Being the root of all, His birth is unknown.

791. Sundara: *Of Unequalled Handsomeness*

ॐ सुन्दराय नमः

His graceful handsomeness is unequalled as He possesses charm, transcending all.

792. Sunda: *Of Melting Nature*

ॐ सुन्दाय नमः

He is very compassionate.

793. Ratnanabha: *Of Beautiful Navel*

ॐ रत्ननाभाय नमः

His navel is to be seen like a jewel.

794. Sulochana: *Of Charming Eyes*

ॐ सुलोचनाय नमः

He has brilliant and charming eyes that are ever watchful.

795. Arka: *The Adored*

ॐ अर्काय नमः

He is adored even by Brahma and others.

796. Vajasana: *The Giver Of Food*

ॐ वाजसनाय नमः

He gives food in abundance to the needy.

797. Shrungi: *The Horned*

ॐ श्रृङ्गिणे नमः

As a fish with horns during the time of Dissolution, He guides the world.

798. Jayanta: *The Conqueror*

ॐ जयन्ताय नमः

He is always the triumphant conqueror of enemies. Or, He is the cause of the victory of the gods.

799. Sarvavijjayi: *The Omniscient And Victorious*

ॐ सर्वविज्जयिने नमः

He conquers internal foes like desire, etc., and external foes like Hiranyakashipu.

800. Suvarnabindu: *With Radiant Golden Limbs*

ॐ सुवर्णबिन्दवे नमः

His *bindus* (limbs) are radiant like gold. Or, He is of the nature of the sound symbol 'Om'.

801. Akshobhya: *The Unruffled*

ॐ अक्षोभ्याय नमः

He remains unruffled by desires, etc., by the objects of the senses, etc., and by the foes of gods, etc.

802. Sarvavigishwareshwara: *The Lord Of The Lords Of Speech*

ॐ सर्ववागीश्वरेश्वराय नमः

He is the Lord of Brahma and others who are lords of speech.

803. Mahahrada: *The Deep Waters*

ॐ महाह्रदाय नमः

The yogins immerse themselves in the deep waters of Bliss which is Lord Vishnu.

804. Mahagarta: *The Great Chasm*

ॐ महागर्ताय नमः

His maya, which is like a great chasm, is difficult to cross.

805. Mahabhuta: *The Great Being*

ॐ महाभूताय नमः

Unlimited by time—past, present and future—He is the great Being.

806. Mahanidhi: *The Great Treasure-house*

ॐ महानिधये नमः

He is the great storehouse in whom the great elements have their support.

807. Kumuda: *One Who Gladdens The Earth*

ॐ कुमुदाय नमः

He relieves the earth of its burden of wicked people and thus gladdens the earth.

808. Kundara: *The Bestower Of Blessings As Pure As Jasmine*

ॐ कुन्दराय नमः

He bestows rewards that are as pure as the *kunda* (jasmine) flower.

809. Kunda: *Pure Like The Kunda*

ॐ कुन्दाय नमः

He is beautiful and pure like the *kunda* (jasmine) flower.

810. Parjanya: *The Rain-cloud*

ॐ पर्जन्याय नमः

He, like the cloud, extinguishes the three miseries arising from psychological, material and spiritual causes. Or, He showers all desired objects like rain.

811. Pavana: *The Purifier*

ॐ पावनाय नमः

Merely by remembering Him, one gets purified.

812. Anila: *The Non-enforcer*

ॐ अनिलाय नमः

Being without any inducement, He is ever awake and omniscient. Or, He is easily accessible to His devotees.

813. Amrutasha: *Enjoyer Of Immortality*

ॐ अमृताशाय नमः

Being the source of nectar, He enjoys immortality. Or, Having given the nectar to the gods, He too partook of it.

814. Amrutavapu: *Of Immortal Form*

ॐ अमृतवपुषे नमः

His form is deathless and undecaying.

815. Sarvajna: *The Omniscient*

ॐ सर्वज्ञाय नमः

He is omniscient and all-knower.

816. Sarvatomukha: *Having Faces On All Sides*

ॐ सर्वतोमुखाय नमः

He has eyes, heads and faces everywhere and on all sides.

817. Sulabha: *Easily Attainable*

ॐ सुलभाय नमः

He is capable of being attained by devotion alone, worshipping Him with flowers, leaves, etc.

818. Suvrata: *Of Excellent Vows*

ॐ सुव्रताय नमः

He enjoys pure offerings. Or, He abstains food or offerings during vows.

819. Siddha: *The Perfect*

ॐ सिद्धाय नमः

His objects are always attained, omnipotent and unobstructed by any other will, as His perfection does not depend on others.

820. Shatrujit: *The Conqueror Of Foes*

ॐ शत्रुजिते नमः

He is the conqueror of foes of the gods.

821. Shatrutapana: *The Tormentor Of The Foes*

ॐ शत्रुतापनाय नमः

He torments the foes who are inimical to gods.

822. Nyagrodha: *Who Is Above All*

ॐ न्यग्रोधाय नमः

He is above all, and the source of everything that is manifest. Or, Controlling all beings, He veils Himself by maya.

823. Udumbara: *Transcending The Ether*

ॐ उदुम्बराय नमः

As the supreme cause, He is superior to all. Or, He nourishes the universe in the shape of food, energy, etc.

824. Ashvattha: *The Impermanent Tree*

ॐ अश्वत्थाय नमः

He is the impermanent tree of worldly life which may vanish the next day. Or, He is the holy fig tree, the eternal tree, having its roots above, and branches below.

825. Chanurandhranishudana: *The Slayer Of Chanura*

ॐ चाणूरान्ध्रनिषूदनाय नमः

As Krishna, He slew Chanura who was sent by Kamsa to kill Him.

826. Sahasrarchi: *The Radiator Of Innumerable Rays*

ॐ सहस्रार्चिषे नमः

The innumerable radiant rays of the luminaries, like the sun, have their source in Him.

827. Saptajihva: *The One with the Seven Tongues Of flame*

ॐ सप्तजिह्वाय नमः

In His manifestation as fire, His tongues of flame are Kali (black), Karali (terrific), Manojava (swift as the mind), Sulohita (very red), Sudhumravarna (Purple), Sphulingini (emitting sparks), and Vishwarupi (all-shaped).

828. Saptaidha: *The One With Seven Flames*

ॐ सप्तैधसे नमः

He, as Fire, has seven forms of brilliance.

829. Saptavahana: *The One With Seven Horses*

ॐ सप्तवाहनाय नमः

The Lord, in the form of sun (Surya), has seven horses as His mounts. Or, His horse named Sapta carries Him.

830. Amurti: *The Formless*

ॐ अमूर्तये नमः

He is One without a form, without a body and limbs. Or, He is without limitations of form consisting of mobile or immobile things.

831. Anagha: *The Sinless*

ॐ अनघाय नमः

He is without sins or pains.

832. Achintya: *The Inconceivable*

ॐ अचिन्त्याय नमः

Being Himself the Witness certifying all knowledge, He is inconceivable by any proof. Or, He cannot be thought of in any particular form, as He is different from this expanded universe.

833. Bhayakrut *Who Causes Fear*

ॐ भयकृते नमः

He causes fear to those who take the crooked path. Or, He dispels fear from the minds of His devotees.

834. Bhayanashana: *The Destroyer Of Fear*

ॐ भयनाशनाय नमः

He destroys the fears of the virtuous who follow the rules of Dharma.

835. Anu: *The Subtle*

ॐ अणवे नमः

Being the minutest of all, this subtle Atman is to be known by the mind.

836. Bruhat: *The Great*

ॐ बृहते नमः

He is the mightiest and the biggest, and greater than the great.

837. Krusha: *The Non-material*

ॐ कृशाय नमः

He is not of a gross body, and so He is a non-material Spirit.

838. Sthula: *The Gross*

ॐ स्थूलाय नमः

As He consists of all, and is the inner pervader of all, He is figuratively described as such.

839. Gunabhrut: *The Bearer Of Attributes*

ॐ गुणभृते नमः

In the creative cycle of creation-preservation-dissolution, He supports the attributes — *sattva*, *rajas* and *tamas*.

840. Nirguna: *Who Transcends All Constituents*

ॐ निर्गुणाय नमः

He is pure Consciousness and devoid of or transcends all constituents.

841. Mahan: *The Great*

ॐ महते नमः

As He is eternally pure and all-pervading, He is devoid of any attributes.

106

842. Adhruta: *Unsustained*

ॐ अधृताय नमः

Though He sustains the earth, etc., He Himself is not sustained by any.

843. Swadhruta: *Self-sustained*

ॐ स्वधृताय नमः

He abides in His own glory, and is sustained by Himself.

844. Swasya: *Having A Beautiful Face*

ॐ स्वास्याय नमः

His face has a fascinating beauty, comparable to the colour and the inside of a lotus. Or, From His face emanated the Vedas to instruct man of the fundamental values of life.

845. Pragvamsha: *Of Primeval Race*

ॐ प्राग्वंशाय नमः

The universe, which has come of Him, is not preceded by anything else, whereas, the descendants of others have come after the universe.

846. Vamshavardhana: *The Expander Of The Universe*

ॐ वंशवर्धनाय नमः

He expands or destroys the world system according to His will.

847. Bharabhrut: *The Bearer Of Burden*

ॐ भारभृते नमः

Assuming the form of Adishesha or Ananta, He supports the earth.

848. Kathita: *The Extolled*

ॐ कथिताय नमः

The Vedas describe Him as the supreme or the highest.

849. Yogi: *Realised Through Yoga*

ॐ योगिने नमः

He can be reached only through yoga. Or, Being ever established in His own Self (Paramatma), He is Yogi.

850. Yogisha: *The Lord Of Yogins*

ॐ योगीशाय नमः

Ordinary yogins lag in their progress owing to obstacles, but He is free from such impediments, and hence the Lord of the yogins.

851. Sarvakamada: *The Fulfiller Of All Wishes*

ॐ सर्वकामदाय नमः

He bestows on His devotees all the desired fruits.

852. Ashrama: *The Hermitage*

ॐ आश्रमाय नमः

He is the peaceful hermitage to which the wanderers flock in the forest of samsara.

853. Shramana: *The Tormentor*

ॐ श्रमणाय नमः

He torments those who live with using their disrimination.

854. Kshama: *The Reducer*

ॐ क्षामाय नमः

During Dissolution, He reduces all beings to the state prior to creation.

855. Suparna: *Having Good Leaves*

ॐ सुपर्णाय नमः

He, as the Samsara tree, has excellent leaves in the form of Vedas.

856. Vayuvahana: *Fearing Him, Vayu Sustains*

ॐ वायुवाहनाय नमः

For fear of Him, Vayu sustains all beings.

857. Dhanurdhara: *The Wielder Of The Bow*

ॐ धनुर्धराय नमः

In His incarnation as Rama, He wielded the mighty bow.

858. Dhanurveda: *The Knower Of The Science Of Archery*

ॐ धनुर्वेदाय नमः

In His incarnation as Rama, He was master of the science of archery.

859. Danda: *The Rod Of Justice*

ॐ दण्डाय नमः

He is Discipline among the disciplinarians.

860. Damayita: *The Subduer*

ॐ दमयित्रे नमः

He is the Subduer of Yama, kings and others.

861. Dama: *The Punishment*

ॐ दमाय नमः

He is in the form of punishment inflicted on those who deserve it.

862. Aparajita: *The Unconquered*

ॐ अपराजिताय नमः

He is the Almighty who is beyond defeat.

863. Sarvasaha: *The Expert*

ॐ सर्वसहाय नमः

He is Expert in all His actions. Or, He is adequate to repel enemies. Or, He supports all in His aspect as earth.

864. Niyanta: *The Regulator*

ॐ नियन्त्रे नमः

He regulates all in their respective functions.

865. Aniyama: *The Unrestrained*

ॐ अनियमाय नमः

He, being the restrainer of all, knows no restraints.

866. Ayama: *The Deathless*

ॐ अयमाय नमः

Since He is deathless, Yama has no control over Him. Or, He is to be reached by means of acquiring yoga like Yama and Niyama.

867. Sattvavan: *Possessed Of Sattva*

ॐ सत्त्ववते नमः

He possesses *sattva* like courage, strength, etc.

868. Sattvika: *Established In Sattva*

ॐ सात्त्विकाय नमः

He is chiefly based on the *sattva* quality.

869. Satya: *The True*

ॐ सत्याय नमः

Being the possessor of truth, He is well-disposed to the good.

870. Satyadharmaparayana: *Ever Devoted To Truthfulness And Righteousness*

ॐ सत्यधर्मपरायणाय नमः

He is always devoted to truthfulness and righteousness in their many aspects.

871. Abhipraya: *The Sought-after*

ॐ अभिप्रायाय नमः

He is sought after by those who seek the ultimate values of life. Or, To Him all beings go directly during Dissolution.

872. Priyarha: *Worthy To Receive Loved Things*

ॐ प्रियार्हाय नमः

He is worthy to receive the loved offerings of the virtuous.

873. Arha: *Deserving Worship*

ॐ अर्हाय नमः

He deserves to be worshipped with all the rituals and rites of worship, like offerings, prostration, singing praises of Him, etc.

874. Priyakrut: *The Doer Of Pleasing Deeds*

ॐ प्रियकृते नमः

Not only is He worthy of devoted worship, but He also fulfils the desires of those who worship Him.

875. Pritivardhana: *The Increaser Of Joy*

ॐ प्रीतिवर्धनाय नमः

He enhances the joy of those who worship Him.

876. Vihayasagati: *One Who Has His Abode In The Firmament*

ॐ विहायसगतये नमः

He, as Vishnu, or the Sun, has His abode in the firmament.

877. Jyoti: *The Light*

ॐ ज्योतिषे नमः

He is the supreme Light, shining of His own accord.

878. Suruchi: *Of Good Effulgence*

ॐ सुरुचये नमः

His brilliance is of an attractive nature.

879. Hutabhuk: *The Consumer Of Oblations*

ॐ हुतभुजे नमः

Though the offerings may be made to other deities, He is the real Enjoyer. Or, He protects the offerings.

880. Vibhu: *The All-pervader*

ॐ विभवे नमः

He is everywhere, pervading everything. Or, He is the all-pervader as He is the Lord of the three worlds.

881. Ravi: *The Sun*

ॐ रवये नमः

In the form of the sun, He absorbs all the waters.

882. Virochana: *Of Various Splendours*

ॐ विरोचनाय नमः

He shines in the form of many luminaries.

883. Surya: *The Generator Of Brilliance*

ॐ सूर्याय नमः

He brings forth great splendour. Or, He brings forth all.

111

884. Savita:

ॐ सवित्रे नमः

It is from Him that all the worlds emerge.

885. Ravilochana: *Having The Sun For His Eye*

ॐ रविलोचनाय नमः

His head is fire, while the eyes are the sun and the moon.

886. Ananta: *The Infinite*

ॐ अनन्ताय नमः

He is eternal, all-pervading, and not limited by time, space and substance.

887. Hutabhuk: *The Protector Of The Sacrifice*

ॐ हुतभुजे नमः

He is both the Protector and the Consumer of oblations.

888. Bhokta: *The Enjoyer*

ॐ भोक्त्रे नमः

The insentient Prakriti is the object for His enjoyment. Or, He is the Protector of the universe.

889. Sukhada: *The Bestower Of Bliss*

ॐ सुखदाय नमः

He confers bliss on His devotees in the form of liberation. Or, He is the Destroyer of misery.

890. Naikaja: *Having Numerous Births*

ॐ नैकजाय नमः

He takes numerous manifestations to protect Dharma.

891. Agraja: *The First-born*

ॐ अग्रजाय नमः

He is Hiranyagarbha, born before anything else.

892. Anirvinna: *The Sorrowless*

ॐ अनिर्विण्णाय नमः

He knows no dejection as He has all His desires fulfilled, and He has nothing more to attain.

893. Sadamarshi: *The Ever-forgiver*

ॐ सदामर्षिणे नमः

He always forgives the virtuous.

894. Lokadhisthanam: *The Basis Of The Worlds*

ॐ लोकाधिष्ठानाय नमः

He is the Basis in whom rest the three worlds.

895. Adbhuta: *The Wonderful*

ॐ अद्भुताय नमः

One sees Him like a wonder, because of His form, power, action, etc.

896. Sanat: *Of Long Duration*

ॐ सनान्मः नमः

Time is the manifestation of the supreme Being, indicating a great length of time.

897. Sanatanatama: *The Most Ancient*

ॐ सनातनतमाय नमः

Being the cause of all, He is older than the most ancient.

898. Kapila: *The Tawny*

ॐ कपिलाय नमः

He has the colour of the subterranean fire which is light red.

899. Kapi: *The Sun*

ॐ कपये नमः

As the sun, He absorbs all the water by His rays. Or, He is Varaha, the boar, in an incarnation.

900. Apyaya: *The Resting Place*

ॐ अप्ययाय नमः

During Dissolution, He is the resting place.

901. Swastida: *The Bestower Of Blessings*

ॐ स्वस्तिदाय नमः

He bestows blessings on His devotees.

902. Swastikrut: *The Doer Of Good*

ॐ स्वस्तिकृते नमः

He does good to the devotees and causes them to do good.

903. Swasti: *The Auspicious*

ॐ स्वस्तये नमः

His nature is auspicious for He is supreme Bliss.

904. Swastibhuk: *The Enjoyer Of Bliss*

ॐ स्वस्तिभुजे नमः

He enjoys supreme Bliss. Or, He enables His devotees to enjoy blessings.

905. Swastidakshina: *Who Grows In Auspiciousness*

ॐ स्वस्तिदक्षिणाय नमः

He augments as auspiciousness. Or, He is adept in conferring auspiciousness. Or, He alone is capable of conferring it. Or, Everything is achieved merely by remembering Him.

906. Araudra: *Devoid Of Wrath*

ॐ अरौद्राय नमः

He is free of *araudra* which is action-desire-anger, all of which are violent.

907. Kundali: *In The Form Of Adishesha*

ॐ कुण्डलिने नमः

He is in the form of Adishesha in its coiled stage. Or, He wears earrings as bright as the sun. Or, He has Samkhya and Yoga, which are fish-shaped, as His ear-pendants.

114

908. Chakri: *The Bearer Of Discus*

ॐ चक्रिणे नमः

He bears the discus called Sudarshana, representing the principle of mind for protecting the worlds.

909. Vikrami: *Endowed With Prowess*

ॐ विक्रमिणे नमः

He is endowed with great prowess. Or, He has the unique movement of His feet. He is thus distinguished from all others.

910. Urjitashasana: *Of Powerful Commands*

ॐ ऊर्जितशासनाय नमः

The *shruti* and *smriti* are His powerful commands.

911. Shabdatiga: *Transcending Speech*

ॐ शब्दातिगाय नमः

His supreme abode is that which transcends speech and is meditated upon by yogins.

912. Shabdasaha: *The Purport Of All Vedas*

ॐ शब्दसहाय नमः

All the Vedas with one intent proclaim or describe Him.

913. Shishira: *The Cool Season*

ॐ शिशिराय नमः

He is the cool refuge to those who are scorched by physial, mental and supernatural torments.

914. Sharvarikara: *The Maker Of Night*

ॐ शर्वरीकराय नमः

The Lord is *sharvari* (night) for those in bondage, and for an enlightened soul, the state of samsara is like night.

915. Akrura: *One Without Cruelty*

ॐ अक्रूराय नमः

Since all His desires are fulfilled, He has no anger or cruelty.

916. Peshala: *Handsome*

ॐ पेशलाय नमः

He is very handsome as His mind, body, deeds, words are all so beautiful.

917. Daksha: *The Skilful*

ॐ दक्षाय नमः

He is skilful, for strength, immensity and quick execution are established in Him.

918. Dakshina: *The Efficient*

ॐ दक्षिणाय नमः

He is as efficient as He is skilful. Or, He pervades everywhere and destroys everything.

919. Kshaminam Vara: *The Chief Among Patient Ones*

ॐ क्षमिणां वराय नमः

He is the chief among the yogins who have forbearance. Or, He is the foremost among those who patiently bear the burden of the earth and all heavenly bodies. Or, He is omnipotent and capable of doing everything, hence the epithet.

920. Vidwattama: *The Wisest*

ॐ विद्वत्तमाय नमः

He alone has the most wonderful knowledge by which He knows everything.

921. Vitabhaya: *The Fearless*

ॐ वीतभयाय नमः

He is free from the fear of transmigratory life.

922. Punyashravanakirtana: *Whose Name, Recited And Heard, Leads To Merits*

ॐ पुण्यश्रवणकीर्तनाय नमः

He who hears this hymn and recites it, will surely be meritorious.

116

923. Uttarana: *The Saviour*

ॐ उत्तारणाय नमः

He saves the devotees from the ocean of worldly life.

924. Dushkritha: *The Destroyer Of Evil Deeds*

ॐ दुष्कृतिघ्ने नमः

He destroys sins or evil deeds.

925. Punya: *The Holy*

ॐ पुण्याय नमः

He bestows holiness on those who remember Him. Or, He enables one to be righteous by teaching the *shrutis* and *smritis*.

926. Duhswapnashana: *The Dispeller Of Nightmares*

ॐ दुःस्वप्ननाशनाय नमः

He dispels bad dreams that forebode coming evils, when He is meditated upon and worshipped.

927. Viraha: *The Bestower Of Salvation*

ॐ वीरघ्ने नमः

He bestows salvation on deserving beings, thus saving them from various transmigratory lives.

928. Rakshana: *The Protector*

ॐ रक्षणाय नमः

By assuming the *sattva* quality, He protects the three worlds.

929. Santa: *The Good*

ॐ सद्भ्यो नमः

The Lord manifests Himself as good beings for spreading excellence and increasing knowledge.

930. Jivana: *The Sustainer Of Life*

ॐ जीवनाय नमः

He sustains the lives of all beings as Prana.

931. Paryavasthita: *The Constant Pervader*

ॐ पर्यवस्थिताय नमः

He remains pervading the whole universe.

932. Anantarupa: *Of Infinite Forms*

ॐ अनन्तरूपाय नमः

Assuming innumerable forms, He resides in the all-comprehending universe.

933. Anantashri: *Of Infinite Power*

ॐ अनन्तश्रिये नमः

He possesses various shaktis, and hence has infinite power.

934. Jitamanyu: *The Conqueror Of Anger*

ॐ जितमन्यवे नमः

He has no anger.

935. Bhayapaha: *The Destroyer Of Fear*

ॐ भयापहाय नमः

He destroys the fears of His devotees from samsara.

936. Chaturashra: *The Just*

ॐ चतुरश्राय नमः

He bestows on the beings the fruits of their karma.

937. Gabhiratma: *Of Immeasurable Self*

ॐ गभीरात्मने नमः

His nature is unfathomable.

938. Vidisha: *The Bestower Of Diverse Fruits*

ॐ विदिशाय नमः

He bestows various fruits on deserving persons for their diverse acts.

939. Vyadisha: *The Director*

ॐ व्यादिशाय नमः

He gives directions and commands to Indra and others according to their functions.

940. Disha: *The Giver*

ॐ दिशाय नमः

He gives all the results of actions through the Vedas.

941. Anadi: *The Beginningless*

ॐ अनादये नमः

Since He is the cause of all, He has no beginning.

942. Bhuvobhuva: *The Support Of the Earth*

ॐ भुवोभुवे: नमः

He is the support of even the earth which supports all.

943. Lakshmi: *The Resplendent*

ॐ लक्ष्मै नमः

He is the splendour of the earth which He supports. Or, He gives the knowledge of the Atman to all beings.

944. Suvira: *Of Auspicious Movements*

ॐ सुवीराय नमः

He has various auspicious movements towards the heart of yogins, the sun's disc, the milky ocean, etc.

945. Ruchirangada: *Adorned With Beautiful Bracelets*

ॐ रुचिराङ्गदाय नमः

He has two beautiful bracelets adorning His arm.

946. Janana: *The Creator*

ॐ जननाय नमः

He creates all beings.

947. Janajanmadi: *The Primeval Cause Of Beings*

ॐ जनजन्मादये नमः

He is the root cause of beings that come to have embodiment.

948. Bhima: *The Source Of Fear*

ॐ भीमाय नमः

He is the cause of fear to those who defy Him.

949. Bhimaparakrama: *Of Fearful Prowess*

ॐ भीमपराक्रमाय नमः

In His incarnations He is feared by the demons for His prowess.

950. Adharanilaya: *The Support Of the Supporter*

ॐ आधारनिलयाय नमः

He supports the five elements which support all.

951. Adhata: *One Requiring No Support*

ॐ अधात्रे नमः

He is supported by His Self, and requires no support. Or, He consumes all during Dissolution.

952. Pushpahasa: *The Blossom Of The Universe-flower*

ॐ पुष्पहासाय नमः

Just like the bud blossoms forth, so has He blossomed as the universe.

953. Prajagara: *The Ever-awake*

ॐ प्रजागराय नमः

Being eternal Awareness, He is not subject to sleep as a result of nescience.

954. Urdhvaga: *The Uppermost*

ॐ ऊर्ध्वगाय नमः

He stays ahead and above all beings.

955. Satpathachara: *The Follower Of Righteousness*

ॐ सत्पथाचाराय नमः

He follows the conduct of the good, walking in the path of righteousness.

956. Pranada: *The Life-giver*

ॐ प्राणदाय नमः

He revives the dead back to life, like in the case of Parikshit.

957. Pranava: *The Supreme Syllable*

ॐ प्रणवाय नमः

He is the supreme Syllable 'Om' denoting the Paramatman.

958. Pana: *Who Has Dealings*

ॐ प्रणाय नमः

He bestows the fruits of karma on all according to their merits.

959. Pramanam: *Wisdom*

ॐ प्रमाणाय नमः

He is Wisdom, or pure Consciousness, which is self-shining in Him.

960. Prananilaya: *The Resting Place Of Prana*

ॐ प्राणनिलयाय नमः

He is the abode or dissolving ground of the Pranas. Or, In Him the prana or being merges. Or, He withdraws the beings during Dissolution.

961. Pranabhrut: *The Sustainer Of Prana*

ॐ प्राणभृते नमः

He sustains beings by means of food.

962. Pranajivana: *The Life Of Beings*

ॐ प्राणजीवनाय नमः

He keeps the beings alive by means of *Prana* or vital life.

963. Tattvam: *The Reality*

ॐ तत्त्वाय नमः

He is Brahman, the real Truth.

964. Tattvavit: *The Knower Of The Truth*

ॐ तत्त्वविदे नमः

Being the basic principle of all *tattvas*, He knows the Truth.

965. Ekatma: *The One Self*

ॐ एकात्मने नमः

He is the sole Being and Atma in all.

121

966. Janmamrityujaratiga: *The Transcender Of All*

ॐ जन्ममृत्युजरातिगाय नमः

He transcends birth, death and decay, for He is not born and never dies.

967. Bhurbhuvasvastaru: *The Essence Of The Vedas*

ॐ भूर्भवः स्वस्तरवे नमः

The three Vyahritis—*Bhuj, Bhuvah, Svah*—are the essence of the Vedas, and men transcend the three worlds with these words. So the Lord is known by these three words. Or, as a tree spreads, He spreads over the three worlds of *bhur, bhuvas* and *svar*.

968. Tara: *The Rescuer*

ॐ ताराय नमः

He rescues the virtuous from the ocean of samsara.

969. Savita: *The Father*

ॐ सवित्रे नमः

As the Father of all, He generates all the worlds.

970. Prapitamaha: *The Great Grandsire*

ॐ प्रपिताहाय नमः

Brahma is the grandfather of all, and Lord Vishnu, the father of Brahma, hence becomes the great Grandsire.

971. Yajna: *In The Form Of Sacrifice*

ॐ यज्ञाय नमः

He is in the form of sacrifice.

972. Yajnapati: *The Lord Of Sacrifices*

ॐ यज्ञपतये नमः

He is the Lord and Protector of sacrifices.

973. Yajva: *The Sacrificer*

ॐ यज्वने नमः

He manifests as the performer of a sacrifice.

974. Yajnanga: *Having The Sacrifices As His Limbs*

ॐ यज्ञाङ्गाय नमः

In His incarnation as the Boar, the sacrifices are His limbs, the sacrificial rites having the Vedas, the post, rites, fire, etc.

975. Yajnavahana: *The Carrier Of Sacrifices*

ॐ यज्ञवाहनाय नमः

He supports the sacrifices that yield various fruits.

976. Yajnabhrut: *The Upholder Of The Sacrifices*

ॐ यज्ञभृते नमः

He upholds and protects the sacrifices.

977. Yajnakrut: *The Creator Of Sacrifices*

ॐ यज्ञकृते नमः

He creates sacrifices or destroys them at the end of the universe.

978. Yajni: *The Goal Of Sacrifice*

ॐ यज्ञिने नमः

He is the whole of which the sacrificers are only parts.

979. Yajnabhuk: *The Enjoyer Of Sacrifice*

ॐ यज्ञभुजे नमः

As the Lord, He is the enjoyer of sacrifices. Or, He is the Protector of them.

980. Yajnasadhana: *Reaching Him Through Sacrifice*

ॐ यज्ञसाधनाय नमः

The sacrifice is the means to reach Him.

981. Yajnantakrut: *The Giver Of The Result Of The Sacrifice*

ॐ यज्ञान्तकृते नमः

He gives the fruits of sacrifice.

982. Yajnaguhyam: *The Secret Of Sacrifice*

ॐ यज्ञगुह्याय नमः

He is the sacrifice of knowledge which is the most esoteric of all the sacrifices.

983. Annam: *The Food*

He is the sustaining power in the food that is consumed by beings. Or, He consumes all during Dissolution.

984. Annada: *The Consumer Of Food*

He is the consumer of the whole universe in the shape of food. He is also *Anna*, the food consumed.

985. Atmayoni: *The Self As Cause*

There is no material cause for the universe other than Himself.

986. Swayamjata: *The Self-born*

He is both the material cause and the instrumental cause of the universe, as He is Self-born.

987. Vaikhana: *The Digger*

In the incarnation of the boar, He dug up the earth and killed Hiranyakashipu.

988. Samagayana: *The Singer Of Samans*

He sings or chants the Samaveda chants.

989. Devakinandana: *The Son Of Devaki*

In His incarnation as Krishna, He was the son of Devaki.

990. Srashta: *The Creator*

He is the Creator of all the worlds.

991. Kshitisha: *The Lord Of The Earth*

ॐ क्षितीशाय नमः

He is the Lord of the earth. Here, 'He' denotes Rama.

992. Papanashana: *The Destroyer Of Sins*

ॐ पापनाशनाय नमः

When anyone meditates upon Him, or worships or remembers Him, He erases his sins.

993. Shangabrut: *The Bearer Of The Conch-shell*

ॐ शङ्गभृते नमः

He wields the conch-shell called Panchajanya which represents the five elements, ego and the rest.

994. Nandaki: *Bearing The Sword Nandaka*

ॐ नन्दकिने नमः

He has the sword called Nandaka, which represents knowledge.

995. Chakri: *The Bearer Of The Discus*

ॐ चक्रिणे नमः

He has the discus called Sudarshana, which represents the mind principle. Or, He turns the wheel of the samsara.

996. Sharngadhanva: *The Bearer Of The Bow*

ॐ शार्ङ्गधन्वने नमः

He has the bow called Sharnga, representing the senses and egotism.

997. Gadadhara: *The Bearer Of The Club*

ॐ गदाधराय नमः

He has the mace called Kaumodaki, representing the principle of intellect.

998. Rathangapani: *With Discus In Hand*

ॐ रथाङ्गपाणये नमः

He carries the Sudarshana in one hand.

999. Akshobhya: *The Imperturbable*

ॐ अक्षोभ्याय नमः

Armed with all the weapons, He is unassailable.

1000. Sarvapraharanayudha: *Armed With Various Striking Weapons*

ॐ सर्वप्रहरणायुधाय नमः

He is armed with various weapons, including His nails (Narasimha avatara), with which He strikes.